Essential Series

Sprin

London
Berlin
Heidelberg
New York
Barcelona
Hong Kong
Milan
Paris
Singapore
Tokyo

Also in this series:

John Cowell
Essential Visual Basic 5.0 *fast*
3-540-76148-9

Duncan Reed and Peter Thomas
Essential HTML *fast*
3-540-76199-3

John Hunt
Essential JavaBeans *fast*
1-85233-032-5

John Vince
Essential Virtual Reality *fast*
1-85233-012-0

John Cowell
Essential Visual J++ 6.0 *fast*
1-85233-013-9

John Cowell
Essential Java 2 *fast*
1-85233-071-6

John Cowell
Essential Visual Basic 6.0 *fast*
1-85233-071-6

Ian Chivers
Essential Visual C++ 6.0 *fast*
1-85233-170-4

John Vince
Essential Computer Animation *fast*
1-85233-141-0

Aladdin Ayesh
Essential Dynamic HTML *fast*
1-85233-626-9

David Thew
Essential Access 2000 *fast*
1-85233-295-6

Ian Palmer
Essential Java 3D *fast*
1-85233-394-4

Matthew Norman

Essential ColdFusion *fast*

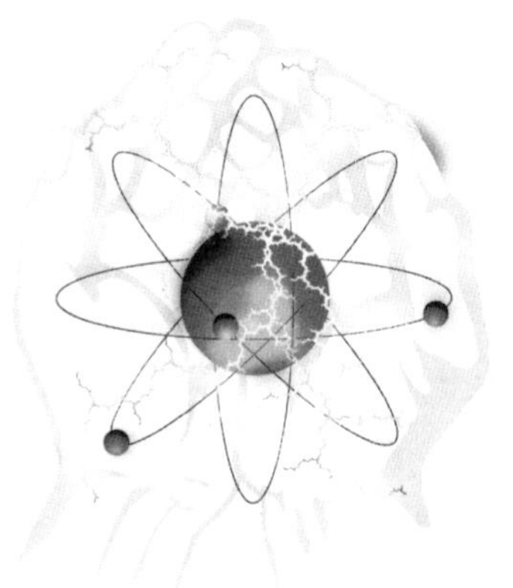

Developing Web-Based Applications

Springer

Matthew Norman, BSc (Hons)
matthew@coldfusionfast.com

Series Editor
John Cowell, BSc (Hons), MPhil, PhD
Department of Computer Science, De Montfort University, The Gateway,
Leicester LE1 9BH

British Library Cataloguing in Publication Data
Norman, Matthew
Essential ColdFusion fast: : developing Web-based
applications - (Essential series)
1. ColdFusion (Computer file) 2. Web sites - Design
I. Title II. ColdFusion fast
005.7'58
ISBN 1852333154

Library of Congress Cataloging-in-Publication Data
Norman, Matthew, 1968-
Essential ColdFusion fast: : developing Web-based applications / Matthew Norman
p. cm. — (Essential series)
Includes index.
ISBN 1-85233-315-4 (alk. paper)
1. Web databases. 2. Database design. 3. ColdFusion (Computer file) I. Title. II.
Essential series (Springer-Verlag)

QA76.9.W43 N67 2001
005.75'8—dc21 00-069841

ISBN 1-85233-315-4 Springer-Verlag London Berlin Heidelberg
A member of BertelsmannSpringer Science+Business Media GmbH
http://www.springer.co.uk

Printed in Great Britain

Typesetting: Camera-ready by author
Printed and bound at The Cromwell Press, Trowbridge, Wiltshire
34/3830-543210 Printed on acid-free paper SPIN 10766551

Contents

Chapter 1

Why Use ColdFusion?

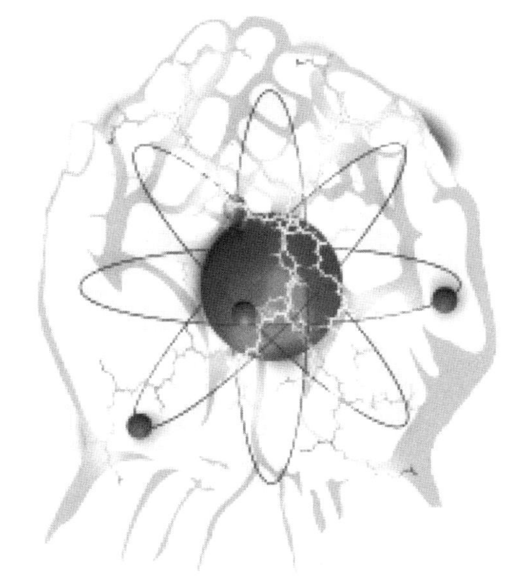

Introduction

ColdFusion is a product that enables you to build interactive web sites easily. The program works in conjunction with a web server on several different operating systems, and will interrogate and manipulate databases and serve the results as web pages. So why is this useful?

Web pages written in HTML allow static pages containing simple information to be viewed, but to write serious, interactive, information rich applications on the web requires an underlying database. ColdFusion allows you to write a web-based application that can connect to such a database.

Perhaps you work in a company that has a huge database of clients. The database is stored on one machine and many people in the company need to look up information about the clients, maybe just for simple uses such as looking up their telephone numbers. Most organizations that have computers and networks have some form of Internet and machines that are capable of using web browsers. So you install an NT box that has a web server, ColdFusion and the database. Users anywhere in the company can now do these simple queries to the database as easily as browsing the web.

This book explains the process of setting up ColdFusion and all of its related technology, through to creating datasources (databases) and web pages. It is assumed that you will have used computer applications such as word processors and web browsers, and have some knowledge of HTML; however, if the user has access to all of the products described, this book will walk you through the whole process.

Is this book for you?

I have written this book because I use and enjoy using ColdFusion, and wish to introduce you to this powerful tool. The ColdFusion documentation supplied with the product is comprehensive, but over 1,000 pages long and so best used as a reference. *Essential ColdFusion* provides you with an introduction which will allow you to develop serious web-based applications which will connect to a database *fast*. It is designed as a quick introduction to ColdFusion and a supplement to these manuals.

The book describes the key features of ColdFusion that will be useful when you are creating your own database-driven web application. Parts of ColdFusion that are not used regularly may not be described in detail in the text.

I have used the Windows platform to develop the code and web servers in this book, but ColdFusion is not only available for this operating system. If you are using another operating system please do not think this book will not be of use. All of the ColdFusion code will be compatible with whatever platform you use. You may, however, have to use other tools to set up the web server and datasources.

If you are about to start a course where you will be using ColdFusion then this book is for you. There are many examples of using ColdFusion and detailed explanations.

If you have read about ColdFusion and want to find if it is the product which meets your needs then read this book. If you also have a connection to the Internet most of the examples can be seen working on the web site described in Chapter 15. If you do not feel like inputting all of the source code, it can be downloaded from the site or from the Essential Series web site at http://*www.essential-series.com*.

If you are thinking about using ColdFusion in your organization then this book will give you a knowledge of how it can be used and what you might need to use it, and you will get some idea of its true potential.

Finally, if you want to set up ColdFusion on a development system, the description in this book should help the process run smoothly.

How this book is organized

If you are about to start using ColdFusion for the first time then working through the book will introduce you to all its facets on a step-by-step basis.

Chapter 2 describes how to set up a typical development system for ColdFusion. Chapter 3 describes a typical ColdFusion application — keeping a log of visitors to a page. Chapter 4 reviews the HTML tags that you will need to write ColdFusion applications. Chapter 5 describes the SQL commands required for referring to databases. If you are already familiar with any of these areas you can move directly to Chapter 6 which looks at ColdFusion in more detail. If you are new to these areas you should read the chapters in sequence, but if you already know an area covered in one of the earlier chapters you can omit it. This book is designed so that the chapters can be read individually. If you are already a ColdFusion user and need to find out about user authentication for example, you can go directly to the chapter where this is covered.

The book does not have worked exercises, but occasionally questions are posed for you. This is intended to get you thinking about using ColdFusion and even to get you writing code yourself. You are encouraged to try and answer these questions where you can. If you totally get stuck you can visit the web site described in Chapter 17 and find the answers there.

Versions of ColdFusion

This book uses ColdFusion 4.5 but the code has been tested on versions 4 and 5 as well. There is no reason, however why this book can not be used with a later or earlier version of the product. You have several options for obtaining a copy of ColdFusion:

- You can buy it. That way you will get the software and the manuals. If you are an educational establishment you may qualify for a reduced price.
- You can buy a copy of ColdFusion Studio, which comes with a developer version of ColdFusion that works on a single machine. ColdFusion Studio is Allaire's HTML editor that also understands all of the ColdFusion functions. This is a much cheaper option than the full server, and includes a good web editor as well.
- You can go to *http://www.allaire.com* and download an evaluation copy of ColdFusion Server which is a time-limited version. If you have a few weeks to concentrate on learning ColdFusion *fast*, this is ideal.
- The Allaire web site also allows you to order a CD full of evaluation products, which contains the same time-limited version but saves you downloading it. At the time of writing this is a free service.
- If you would like to check out the new versions of ColdFusion, you can obtain them by joining the Allaire beta-testing program. Once registered you may download new versions from *http://beta.allaire.com*.
- The Allaire site also has a cut down version of ColdFusion server, ColdFusion Express, which is free to download and the best option if you are on a budget. Be aware that some functions available in the full version may not be included in the free versions.

Most of the functions that are described within this book are available on all of these versions. If something described in the book does not work on your system, first check that your administrator has not disabled the function that you were trying to use. Next have a look at the Allaire site at the comparison between different versions to check if your version supports the function.

If you do not wish to obtain ColdFusion in these ways there is one other option open to you. Several web sites are now offering free ColdFusion hosting. These sites allow you to upload your code and run it on their servers. One of the best currently available can be found at *http://www.freecfm.com*.

ColdFusion 5.0

At time of writing ColdFusion 5.0 is just around the corner. The code in this book has been tested with this version of the software. Most of the differences between versions 4, 4.5 and 5 are all in the more sophisticated features of the software, such as load balancing and clustering – features to allow your servers to share the work and prevent failure. Most users with an interest in the software will not use these features and so they have not been documented in this book.

I hope that you enjoy this book and that it helps you in your work, research or development. Over the four years that I have used ColdFusion it has revitalized my enjoyment of programming and allowed me to make Internet programming much more dynamic and enjoyable. I hope that it can do the same for you.

Chapter

2

Setting up a Development System

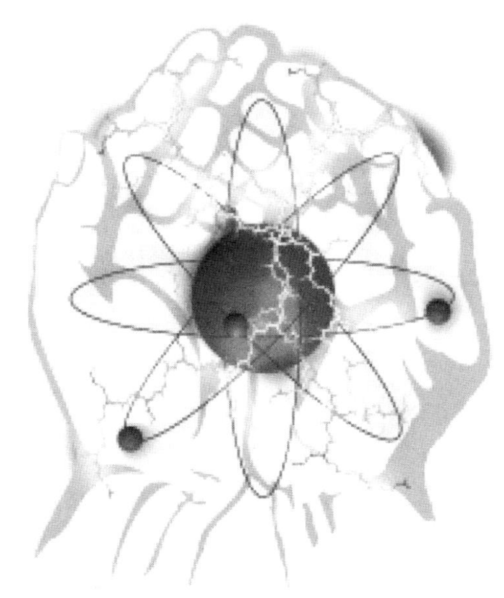

Introduction

This chapter describes what you need and what you have to do to set up a ColdFusion development system on a single PC. Without this, you will not be able to try the examples and gain hands-on experience.

In practice, organizations tend to have a dedicated web server on which to install the software, and separate development machines.

Prerequisites

To create ColdFusion applications you will need the following:

- A PC with Windows 95 or above or NT 4 or above.
- Web Browser Software.
- IIS (Internet Information Server) on NT and Windows 2000 or PWS (Personal Web Server) on Windows 95/8 and Millennium Edition or compatible web server on other non-Windows operating systems.
- Microsoft Access.
- ColdFusion Server software.

The PC

The examples in this book have been developed using a web server that has a 233MMX Intel Pentium processor and 64 megabytes of memory. However, any book that you pick up will have different specifications for a PC, as these change regularly. It is safe to say that the better the specification of machine the better that ColdFusion will run. As our example system is based on the 95/98 platform our specification was adequate but could be improved. If you are going to be using NT you will need at least 128 megabytes of RAM. When the development code is transferred to your live web server that may be running NT, a more up-to-date specification will be needed. You will need a CD drive to install the software, or an Internet connection if you are downloading the trial or limited versions. If you are using a non-Windows operating system check the specification needed as described in the ColdFusion documentation.

Web Browser software

As the whole point of ColdFusion is to design applications for the web, web browser software is required to view the results. Two of the most popular browsers are Netscape Navigator and Microsoft's Internet Explorer but there are others. It is best to use the most up-to-date version of your favourite browser; however, you need to bear in mind that web pages can look different on different browsers, so testing your code on several different versions and types can save embarrassing mistakes later. A good example of this is missing off an end tag from the HTML code. For instance if in your code you have a <TABLE> tag and miss out the </TABLE> to close it, Internet Explorer will render the page correctly; however, on Netscape Navigator all the code will produce is a blank page. So test your code on as many different browsers as you can find.

Web Server software

As mentioned in the previous chapter the ColdFusion application server runs in conjunction with a web server. It requires any server that supports ISAPI, NSAPI, Apache API, or CGI. One of the most common web servers on Windows NT is IIS (Internet Information Server) that probably is popular because it is bundled free with NT.

Another option for a Windows 95 or 98 setup is to use Personal Web Server (PWS). This can be downloaded from the Microsoft web site and is also included on the Windows 98 setup CD. This is what the author uses for development purposes.

Microsoft Access

If your application is to use a database of any kind then there needs to be some method of creating the datasource. One of the easiest ways to do this (if you have Microsoft Office installed) is to use Microsoft Access. Once an empty datasource is created it is possible to add data using SQL statements embedded in your ColdFusion programs (template files). During development it is much easier to quickly open the source in Access and change a table name, or check if data is valid than using any other method.

On the main server MS Office may not be available and MS SQL Server, part of Back Office may be used. If you are not too familiar with SQL and you have Access installed it may make your development easier.

Microsoft Office 2000 uses a different data format for its Access files, so you may wish to check that this is still compatible with the version of ColdFusion that you are using. Refer to Allaire's web site for up-to-date details on this.

There is also the need to make the database available as a data source on the system. This is done by means of ODBC (Open DataBase Connectivity). This process makes a database file available to other processes on the machine. Setting this up is straightforward and will be explained later on.

ColdFusion Server software

Finally you need a copy of the ColdFusion server. The first chapter described the options in greater detail, but in brief

these are:

- Buy the full product.
- Buy ColdFusion Studio and use the single user server included with it.
- Download an evaluation copy from Allaire's web site.
- Order an evaluation CD from Allaire.
- Register and download a beta version.
- Download ColdFusion Express, the free cut-down version.

The Plan

We will now set up a test system. Our system will be on a Windows 98 machine with Microsoft Office installed as well as Internet access (to acquire the necessary networking protocols). A CD-ROM drive is also required. The principles here described will, however, be valid for any test system. The processes involved are:

- Install the web server.
- Install ColdFusion.
- Test ColdFusion.
- Create a database file.
- Register the file as an ODBC datasource.
- Test our datasource through ColdFusion.

Installing the web server

First we need to install PWS (Personal Web Server) onto our Windows 98 machine which we will be using to demonstrate the systems. Place your Windows 98 CD-ROM in the drive. Depending on how you have your system set up, either the install Windows 98 screen will appear as in figure 2.1, or nothing will happen. If the setup screen appears, select the **Browse this CD** option.

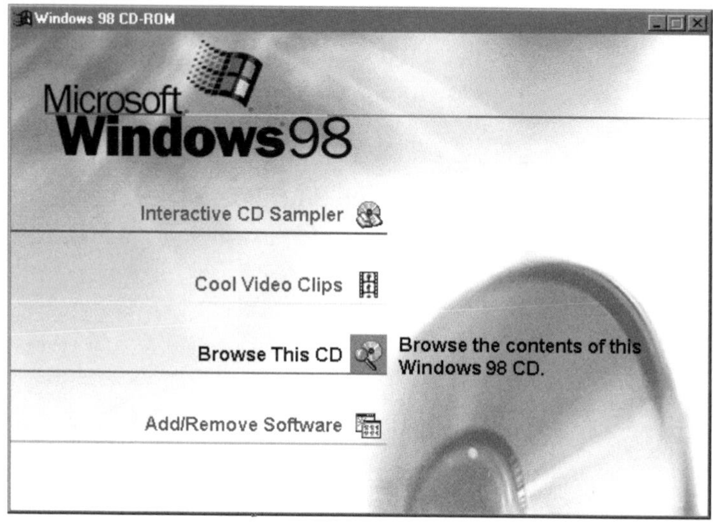

Figure 2.1 – Windows 98 setup screen.

If it does not appear, open up your **My Computer** icon from the desktop, right click with the mouse on your CD drive icon and select **Explore** as in figure 2.2.

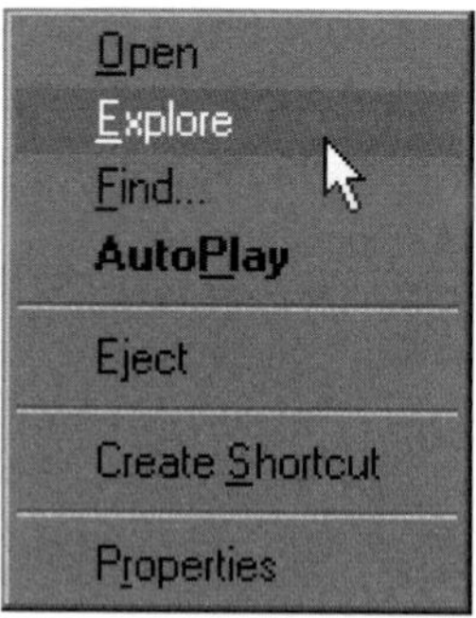

Figure 2.2 – Exploring the CD manually.

You will be presented with a directory structure of the CD, and the file you want to use is in the *add-ons/pws* directory. When you find this you will see quite a few files as in figure 2.3.

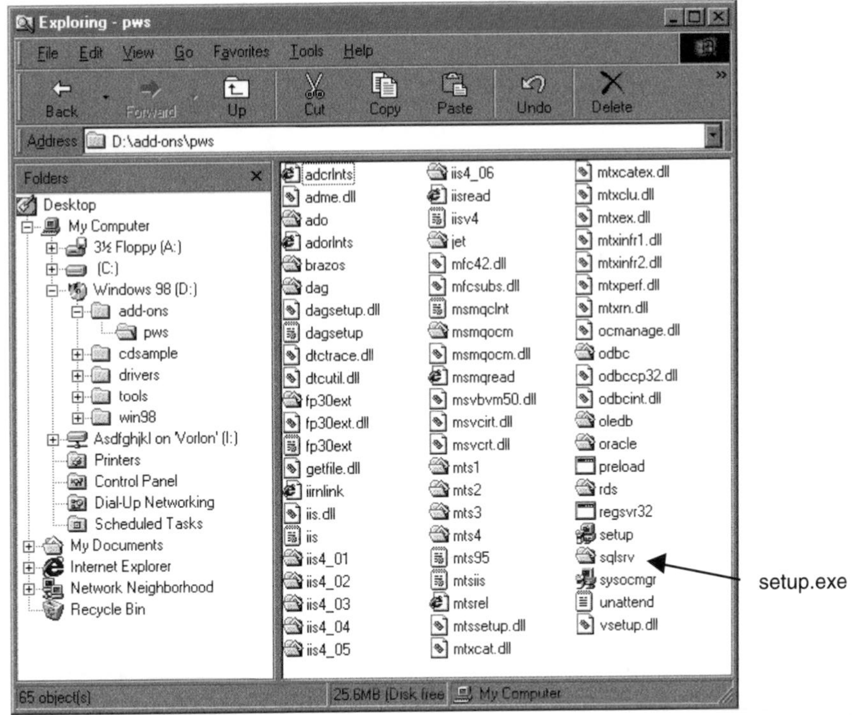

Figure 2.3 – Personal Web Server setup files.

From this directory double click the *setup.exe* file to start your installation. Depending on your version of the software you will be presented with a screen similar to figure 2.4.

You will next be presented with several options for the action; **Minimal, Typical** or **Custom**. Unless you are an experienced user with special requirements choose **Typical**. If you have not installed Internet protocols on your machine at this time you may be prompted to do so.

These protocols are found in the Network Control Panel of your PC, and are called TCP/IP. These are the rules that the computer uses to communicate with the Internet. Once the installation is complete you will probably have to restart your computer, which is something that you will have to get used to in the installation process.

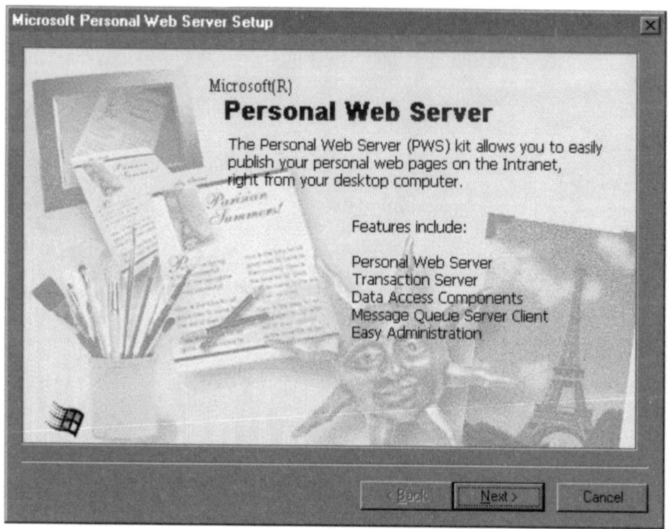

Figure 2.4 – Personal Web Server setup screen.

After restart you will have a new icon in your system tray, on the bottom right of your screen shown in figure 2.5 as the icon between the speaker and the time.

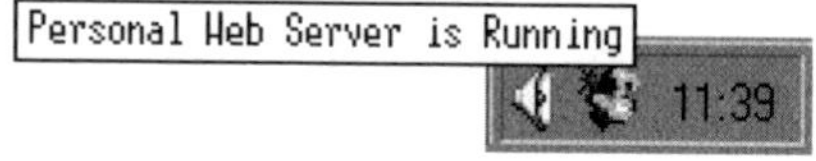

Figure 2.5 – Personal Web Server icon in system tray.

If you move your cursor over this icon the **Personal Web Server is Running** message will appear as in the figure.

This is a good indicator that your installation has been successful. If you right click on the icon you will get a context menu that allows you to adjust the properties of the web server as well as start, stop and pause it.

Next you need to check that the web server is serving web pages. Start your web browser and type the following into the Location or Address box:

```
http://machinename/
```

Type the name of your machine where it says **machinename**. If you do not know this it can be found in the **Control Panel**, **Network Properties** under the **Identification** tag. You may also use the number 127.0.0.1 instead of the name. This is a special TCP/IP number that refers to the local machine you are actually using, sometimes called **localhost**. We will use this number, which will work whatever the name of the machine, in the examples in the rest of this chapter, following this procedure on your computer specifying your own machine name. After you have decided what to type and pressed return, in a few seconds a page shown in figure 2.6 will be displayed. When this appears you have correctly set up your personal web server.

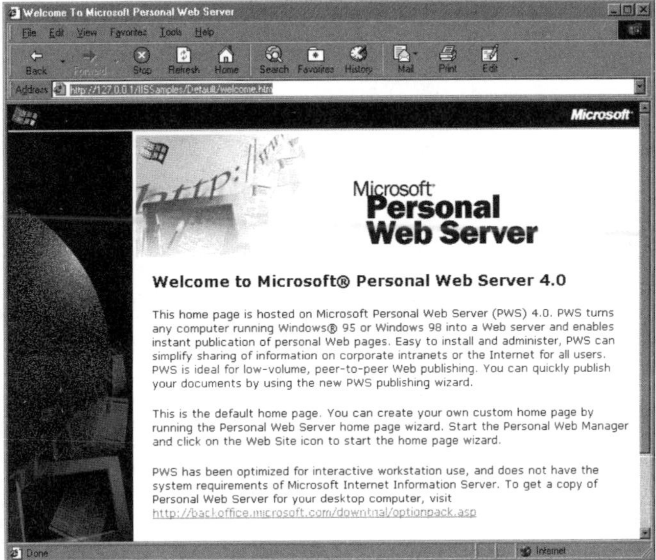

Figure 2.6 – A default Personal Web Server home page.

Installing ColdFusion

Having installed the web server the next step is to install the ColdFusion server. We shall assume that we are installing a full version of ColdFusion from the install CD.

Place this in the drive and if autorun is available on your machine the screen shown in figure 2.7 should appear. If it does not then go to **My Computer**, and double click on your CD drive icon and then on the *setup.exe* file. You will now see figure 2.7.

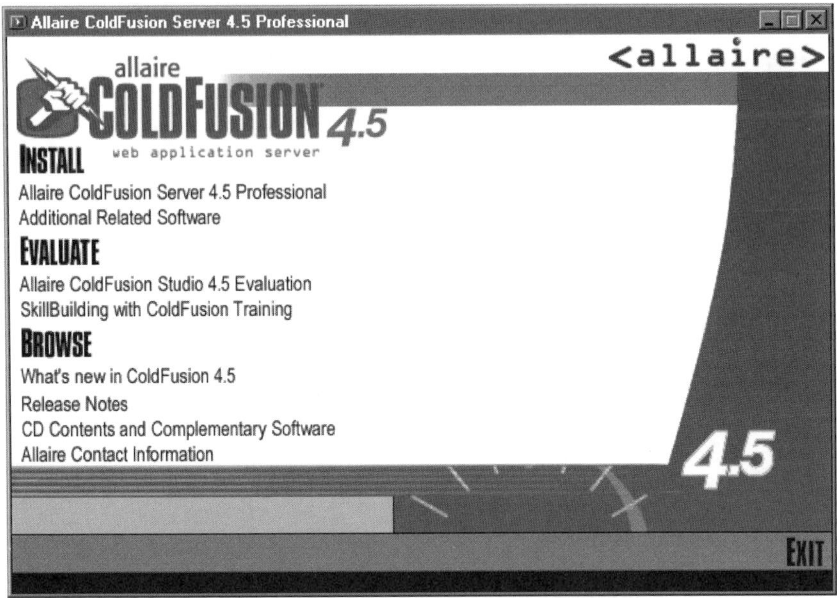

Figure 2.7 – The ColdFusion setup screen.

From the screen shown in figure 2.7 select the Install ColdFusion Server option. After agreeing to the licensing agreement and entering your details and serial number, you will be presented with a prompt asking where you wish to install the server; accept the default path. Next you will be asked which web server you wish to use with ColdFusion. If you are not presented with a Personal Web Server option then you have not installed, or restarted after installing, PWS. Select the option containing Personal Web Server and continue following the prompts and accepting the defaults for:

- Where the web files will be stored.
- The components to be installed.

- The administrator password (Don't forget this; write it down!).
- The shortcut locations.

You will be prompted again to restart the machine; so do this now.

Testing ColdFusion

After the restart, look in the system tray and you will see two new icons as shown in figure 2.8.

***Figure 2.8** – The ColdFusion system tray icons.*

Running the mouse over these in turn reveals that they are called:

- ColdFusion 4.5 IDE service.
- ColdFusion 4.5.

Right clicking on these icons enables you to shut each one down in turn, as well as run the administration options.

Concentrate for the moment on the one that says ColdFusion 4.5 IDE service. Right click, and from the pop up list select ColdFusion Administrator as in figure 2.9.

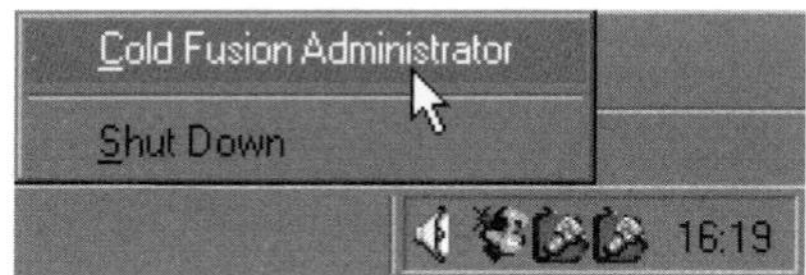

***Figure 2.9** – Selecting from the system tray.*

A web browser will start up and you will get to a screen that prompts for the Administrator password which you entered, and hopefully remembered, during the setup process. Once this is done the form shown in figure 2.10 is displayed.

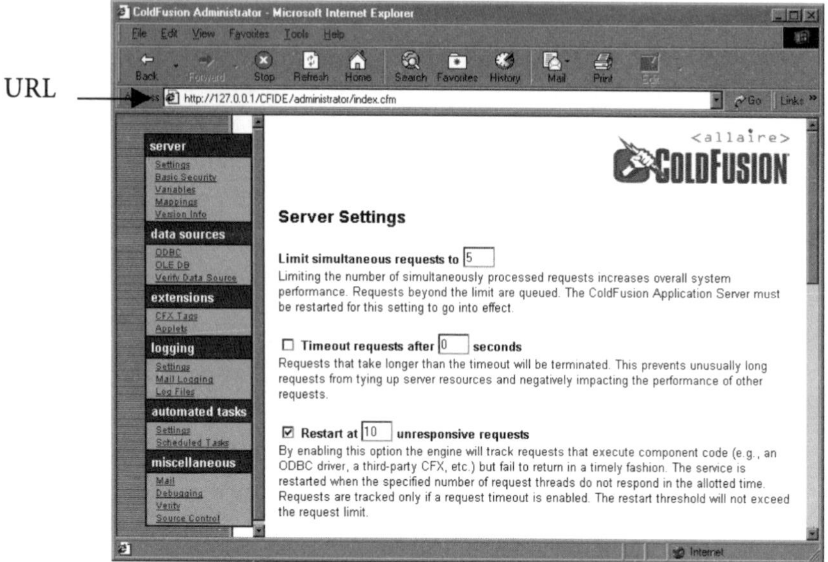

Figure 2.10 – ColdFusion administration page.

Note the URL shown in figure 2.10:

```
http://127.0.0.1/CFIDE/administrator/index.cfm
```

The actual file being viewed is a *.cfm* template file. As the page looks like a normal web page this shows that ColdFusion has successfully parsed the template file and everything is working correctly.

Creating a database file using Access

We need to move away from the web technologies in the next step and create a database that will become a datasource. We can then register this datasource to the system so that ColdFusion can use the data within. Close down anything that you still may have open on your screen.

We will create an Access file that we will use and describe in more detail in the next chapter. For now all this database will do is store data about a user's visit to one of our web pages.

Start Microsoft Access by clicking on the icon or selecting it from the **Start Menu**. You will get the dialog shown in figure 2.11.

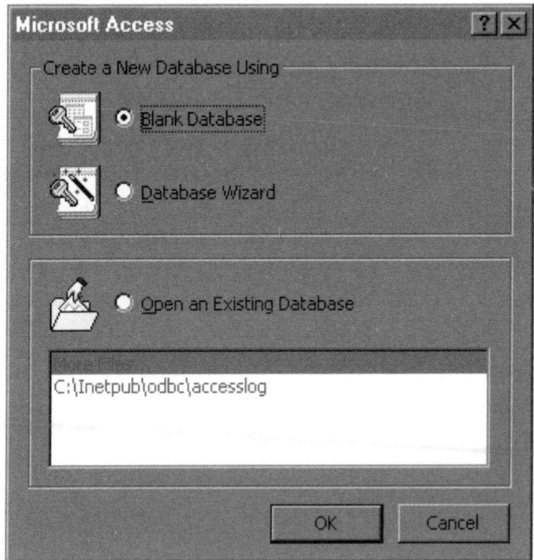

Figure 2.11 *– Starting Microsoft Access.*

As shown in figure 2.11 select the **Blank Database** option of the **Create a New Database** section and click **OK**. You are next asked to provide a filename and a location for your database. Call the database *accesslog.mdb*. When you installed the web server software you were asked for a location for the Internet files which by default is *c:\inetpub*.

In this directory is another directory called *wwwroot*. Anything stored here will be available via the web server. This would cause some serious security problems if the entire Access database was placed here and therefore available to anyone who guesses the name of the file. Imagine the danger of placing such a file in a public place if it contained sensitive information such as credit card details. By placing the file where it cannot be downloaded, you can control exactly the data that you want returned to the user by means of your ColdFusion programming. The file can be stored anywhere on your server's hard drive, but a reasonable place would be in an *odbc* sub-directory off the *inetpub* directory. Place your new Access file there, creating an *odbc* directory first if it does not exist already.

Although it would be possible to create all of the data structure inside the database table using ColdFusion and SQL statements, it is less time consuming at this stage to use Access. After creating your new database you will see the screen shown in figure 2.12. The **Tables** tab should be selected and then the **New** button pressed.

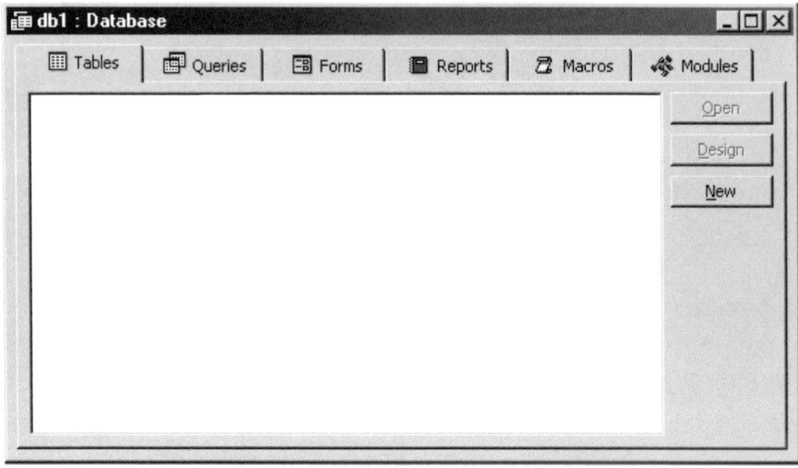

Figure 2.12 *– A blank Access database.*

When you have pressed the **New** button you will be asked how you wish to construct the new table; select design view and click **OK**. You will then be presented with a screen that resembles figure 2.13. This figure shows the data structure of the table that is to be created.

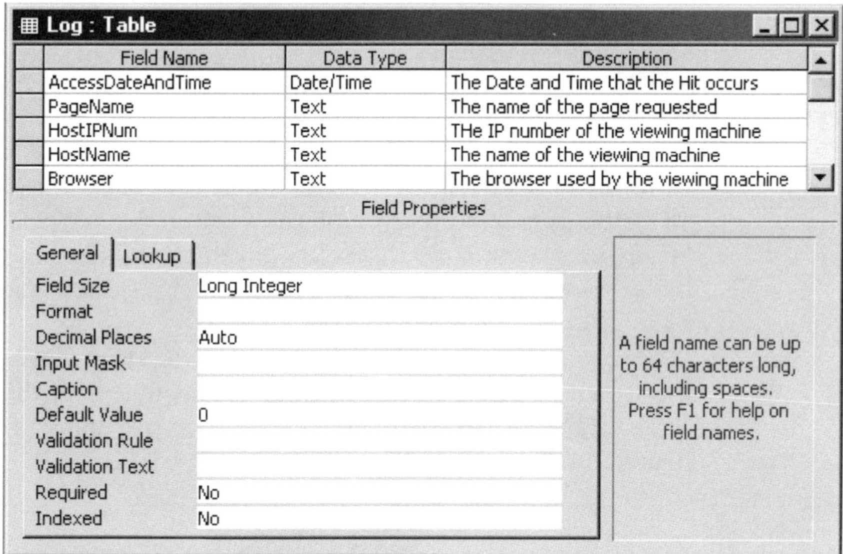

Figure 2.13 *– The Log table implemented in Microsoft Access.*

Enter the field names in the field column as shown in figure 2.13 and below, noting that there are no spaces in the words:

- AccessDateandTime.
- PageName.
- HostIPNum.
- HostName.
- Browser.

Set the *AccessDateandTime* data type to **Date/Time**, all the rest set to **Text**. You can set the description as shown in figure 2.13 for completeness, however this is not mandatory. When you are satisfied with your table click on the **save** icon (the floppy disk on the icon bar) or the cross to turn the design view off. On both occasions you will be asked for a table name. Call your table *Log*. We will refer to this table by name in most of the code in the following chapters, so the correct name is important. Exit Access now that you have finished creating the table.

Registering the file as an ODBC datasource.

Now we have created the database we have to register it as an ODBC source so that ColdFusion can make use of it. From the system tray, right-click on the ColdFusion 4.0 IDE service icon and select ColdFusion Administrator as in figure 2.9.

After entering your Administrator password you will see the screen in figure 2.10. Down the left-hand side of this screen you will see the list of options that are shown in figure 2.14.

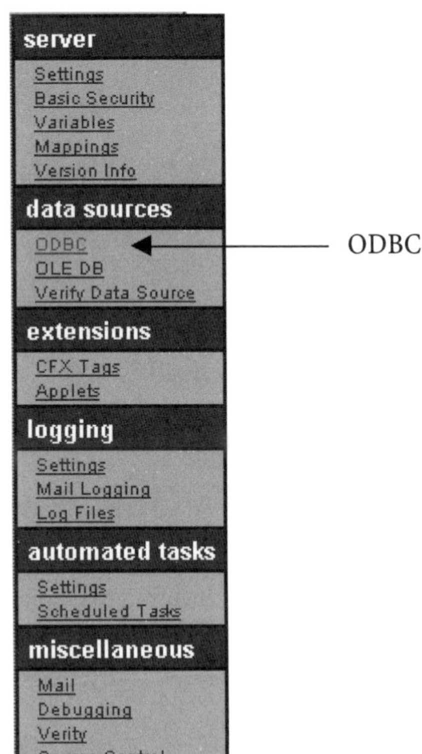

Figure 2.14 – Administrator options.

Figure 2.14 shows the many options that are available to you as the ColdFusion administrator. At this stage most of these can usually be ignored. At present we will only be using the option to set up the ODBC source, so click on the **ODBC** link in the second block of links down. Figure 2.15 shows the screen that appears next.

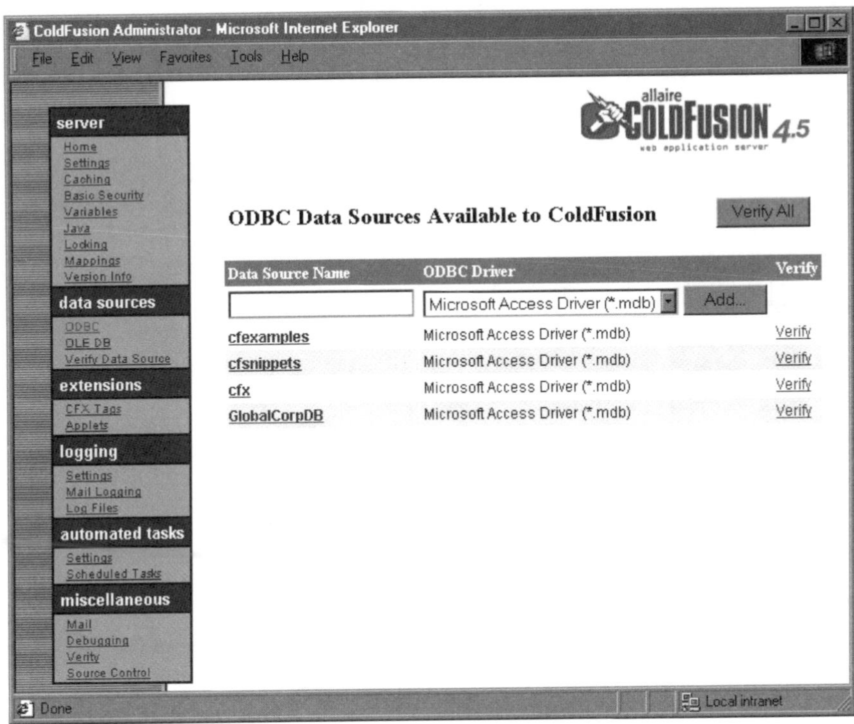

Figure 2.15 – Setting up an ODBC data source: source selection.

In the box under **Data Source Name**, type the name that you wish to use to identify the data source. This will be used in your code later to tell the server where to look for the tables. In the examples in the next chapter we will use the source name *mylog*, so type this in and click on the **Add** button. Figure 2.16 shows the properties screen that appears next.

You will notice that figure 2.16 has an entry in the **Database File** field. To add this, you need to click on the **Browse Server** button next to this field.

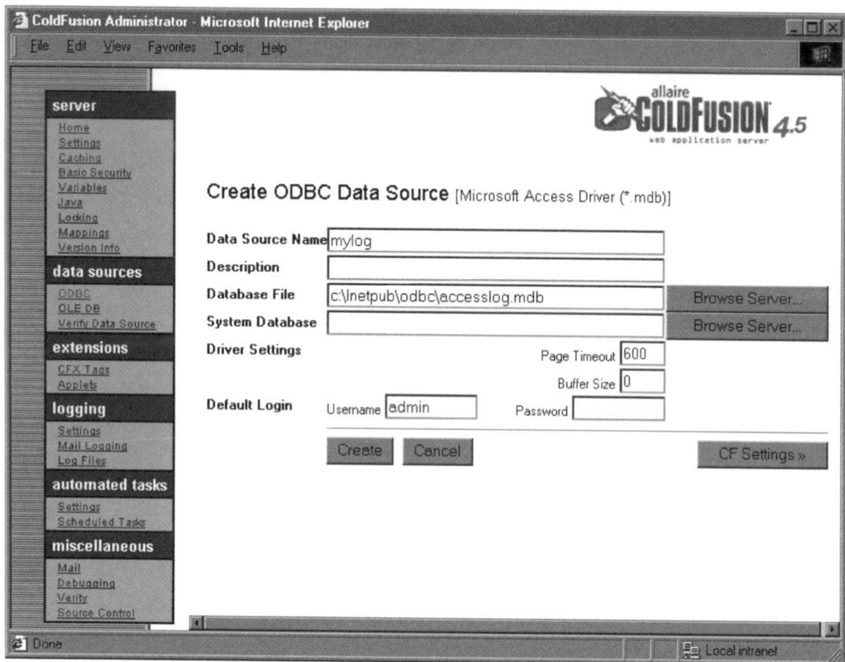

Figure 2.16 - Setting up an ODBC data source: source properties.

The **Browse Server** button will start up a Java application that allows you to select your database file from the server, which if you have been following the instructions in this chapter will be at:

```
c:\Inetpub\odbc\accesslog.mdb
```

If you have stored the database file anywhere else, make sure that you select the correct location for your own setup. Once this file is selected, press the **Create** button and you will be taken back to the screen in figure 2.15 with your new datasource added to the list. You can quickly check this source has been set up correctly by clicking on the verify link on the `mylog` datasource line.

Note **that** this is not the only way to register a ODBC source. It can also be done the following way:

- From the **Start** menu select **Settings/Control Panel.**
- Double click on the **ODBC Data Sources (32 bit)** icon.

- Name and select the source in a similar manner to the way described previously in this chapter.

Testing the installation

To test the datasource, the web server and ColdFusion, type the following into a text editor such as Notepad.

```
<HTML>
<TITLE>A quick test</TITLE>
<BODY>
<CFQUERY datasource="MyLog" name="Hits">
      Select       *
      from  Log
</CFQUERY>
<CENTER>
<H1>Hello world!</H1>
</BODY>
</HTML>
```

Save the above code in your *inetpub\wwwroot* directory calling it *index.cfm*. We can now view this file via a web browser, by typing *http://127.0.0.1/index.cfm* into the address field of your browser.

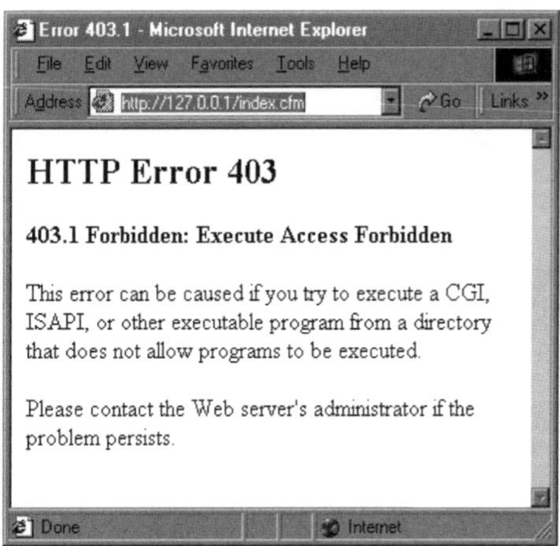

***Figure 2.17** – A 403 Error.*

An error shown in figure 2.17 indicates that there is one last thing do to complete our installation.

The web server now needs to be told the name of every directory that has ColdFusion template files that need to be executed. This is because a web view in such a directory will trigger the ColdFusion executable on the server, and it needs permission from the system to do this.

To set this up we need to look at the Personal Web Server settings as follows:

- Right click on the PWS icon in your system tray.
- From the pop up menu select the **Properties** option, which will show the screen in figure 2.18. From this screen you can start and stop your web server and get to some of the other settings.

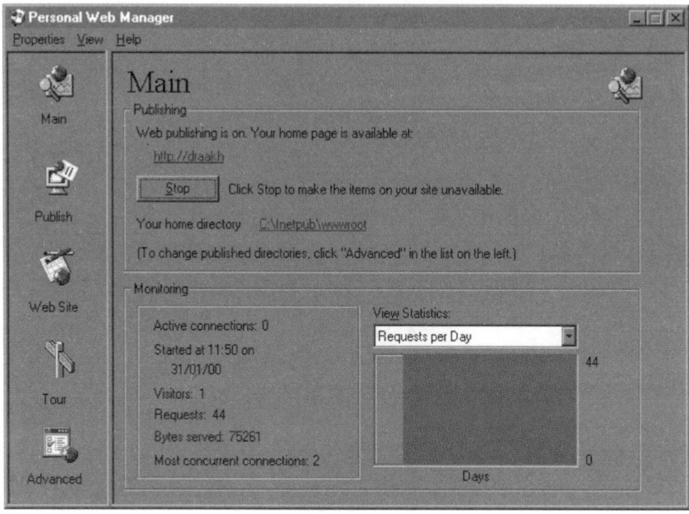

Figure 2.18 – Personal Web Server first setup screen.

- Click on the **Advanced** icon to show the screen in figure 2.19.

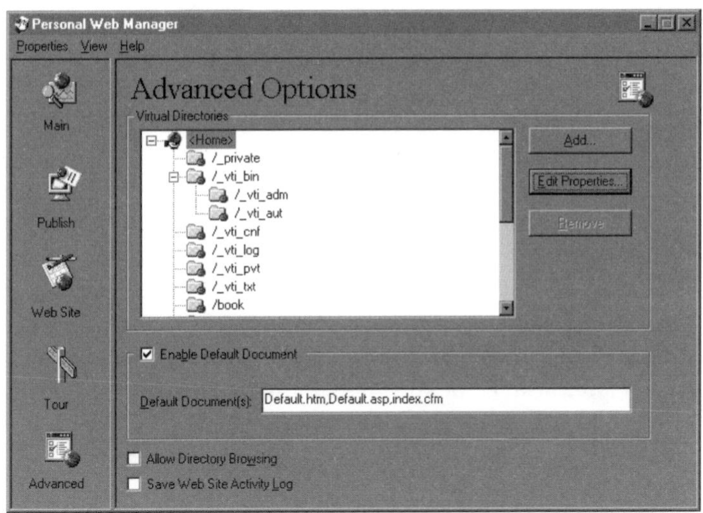

Figure 2.19 – Advanced options in PWS Properties.

- Make sure that the *<HOME>* directory is selected.
- Click on the **Edit Properties** button. The dialogue shown in figure 2.20 appears. This will have the link to your home directory, *c:\inetpub\wwwroot* and several access options.

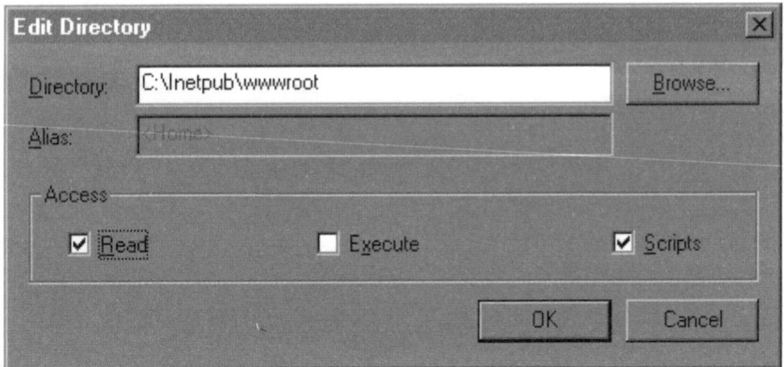

Figure 2.20 – PWS directory properties.

- By default only **Read** and **Scripts** will be checked, so make sure that **Execute** also has a tick by it.
- Click on **OK**, which will return you to the screen in figure 2.19. If you are setting up any other directories on the server with ColdFusion template

files in them, bear in mind that you need to set execute access on these as well.

At this point you may also set the default document options. A default document is the document name that the web server will look for if it receives a request for a directory on the server and not a specific file. The server will then check for a default filename in the directory and display that. By default Personal Web Server looks for *default.htm* and *default.asp* files. It will not look for ColdFusion template files as we have not registered them. Click on the field with these two files in them, and type *index.cfm* before the other two file types, so the line now reads:

```
index.cfm,default.htm,default.asp
```

If prompted for a directory, PWS will now look first for an *index.cfm* file, then a *default.htm* file and finally a *default.asp* file. The set up procedure is now complete. To test it, open your web browser and go to the following URL:

```
http://127.0.0.1/index.cfm
```

This will show a page with nothing other than *Hello World* printed on it. If no other error is displayed, ColdFusion has also performed a simple access to the datasource we set up earlier and we are ready to develop our first application which is described in the next chapter.

Chapter

3

Counting Visitors to a Web Site

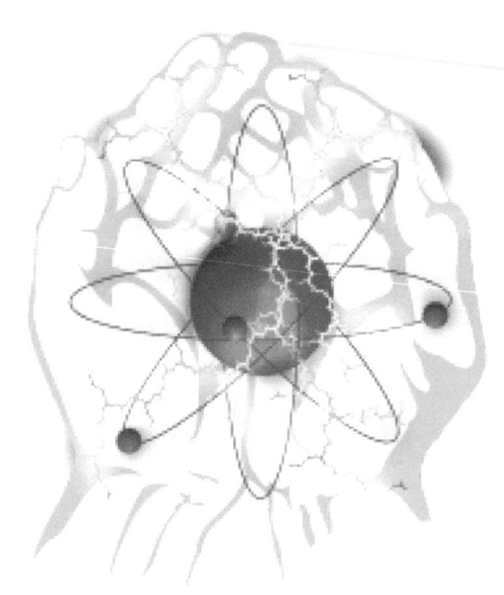

Introduction

As you have been surfing the web, you will notice many similarities between web pages. A common feature on many web sites is the page counter, which logs the number of times that visitors have viewed the site. These can take many forms, from simple numbers to complex graphical output and fonts. Many sites provide small programs that you can add to your web site so that you can join in this counting trend.

In this chapter we will add a page counter 'application' to a web page to keep a record of how many times a page is visited. However, instead of obtaining a counter from a website and blindly using it, we will program one ourselves in ColdFusion as an introduction to some of the concepts involved. This chapter will therefore introduce:

- The ColdFusion template file (*.cfm*).
- The importance of the underlying data structure.
- Running an SQL query (using <CFQUERY>).
- Displaying the results of the SQL query (using <CFOUTPUT>.
- Additional formatting of the output (using tables).

We will be re-visiting many aspects of this application in later chapters, but at this stage it is helpful to be able to see how a complete application is implemented. We start by describing how it could be done in general in HTML.

The HTML way

When you access a web page the counter software increments a variable which represents the number of visitors to that page, or the site. This variable is stored in some way on the server and passed back to the viewer as a number, or a graphical representation of that number.

A basic HTML document that contains a standard page counter is shown below:

```
<HTML>
<TITLE>My Web Page</TITLE>
<BODY> <CENTER>
<H1>My Web Page</H1>
<P>Welcome to my page, glad you could come!
<P>Here is what I look like: <BR><BR>
<IMG src="mugshot.jpg">
<P>You are the <Page counter code>  visitor to this site.</P>
</CENTER>
</BODY>
</HTML>
```

If your HTML is a little rusty then you can review the basics in Chapter 4.

Note the part of the code that reads:

```
<Page Counter Code>
```

If this were valid HTML there would be some method of implementing the page counter at this point in the code. However as we are not going to discuss how to implement this in HTML we will not describe this code.

Figure 3.1 – A Home Page with page counter.

If some code were there, the HTML above produces the page shown in figure 3.1.

Every time that a user looks at this page, the number of this page goes up by one. If you re-load or refresh the page after this occasion, it would read 217.

Our version of this page will look the same but have more hidden functionality. However, in our example we will store details of every access in a database. This will be quite a simple database that could be extended at a later date. We therefore need to continue by describing the data that we are going to store in our application.

The visitor database structure

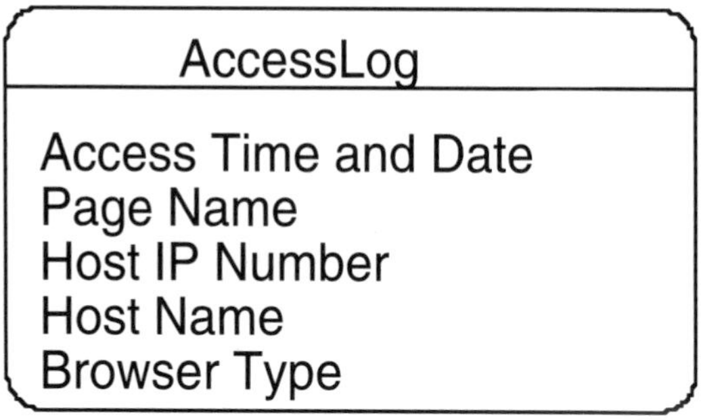

AccessLog

Access Time and Date
Page Name
Host IP Number
Host Name
Browser Type

Figure 3.2 *– Example database structure.*

The database is going to have the structure shown in figure 3.2. The table is called AccessLog, and the list underneath shows the various attributes (or fields) that are stored in each record. The figure simply shows the name of the database table and its fields, which could be created in Microsoft Access or any SQL database.

Not all attributes will be stored at first, but when planning a database it is best to try and anticipate how it might be used in the future. Our example has extra attributes so that more functionality can be added if needed. The current attributes are as follows:

- **Access time and date** – This stores the date and time that the page was viewed. Most databases have a function that stores both the date and time as one object, so this has not been split into two separate attributes.
- **PageName** – This stores the name of the page that the user is looking at. This is not so important with small web sites but as our web site gets bigger it would be useful to have statistics for every individual page viewed.
- **Host IP Number** – This stores the IP number of the machine that is looking at our server. The IP, or Internet Protocol, number is the unique identification number of any machine connected to the Internet. This can be useful for tracking a particular user's path through the site.
- **Host Name** – This is similar to the Host IP Number, but stores the domain name of the machine that is viewing our pages. It can be useful, if the remote machine is registered to a domain, to see where our visitors are from.
- **Browser Type** – This stores the type of web browser that is accessing the page. This could prove useful if certain pages do not work with particular browsers, so we have an opportunity to view some statistics about who is using what, and therefore tailor our web pages to match the most frequently used browsers.

Each time a person looks at our page, the system will store information about the access in the database table. To obtain the page count, the records in the database are counted and the number sent back to the user (who is usually unaware of all the information they have just provided).

Modifying the HTML

We are going to rewrite the HTML code to allow us to use a ColdFusion script inside the page. The first difference between a Hyper Text Markup Language (HTML) file and a ColdFusion Markup Language (CFML) file is the file extension. Normally a file with HTML content would be saved with a *.htm* or *.HTML* extension, for example:

```
index.htm
```

Normally the end user puts in a request for the page with his browser by specifying the URL. The browser then sends this request to the remote web server, that loads in the file from its storage and sends it back as it is to the user's web browser.

If the page had CFML inside it, the file name extension would now be *.cfm*, for example:

```
index.cfm
```

When the web server software receives a request for this type of file, it knows that more is required than the simple transmission of the file back to the user. So instead of sending it directly, it first passes the CFML file (or template file) to the ColdFusion service on the server. The ColdFusion server then executes the ColdFusion instructions contained within the file. The output of this program is HTML code that has been dynamically created based on these instructions. The HTML file is then passed back to the web server, which in turn passes this file back to the end user, who never views the original template file, only the results of its processing.

In addition, the ColdFusion server may have to access a database to generate its results. To access the database, the template file will have Standard Query Language (SQL, sometimes pronounced 'sequel') code inside it.

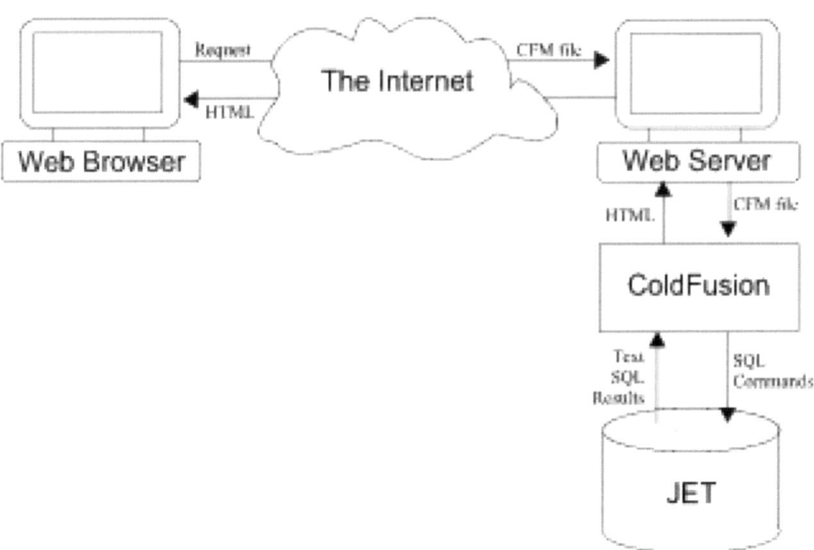

Figure 3.3 – The ColdFusion Process.

Instructions written in SQL are able to interrogate a database. The ColdFusion server passes the SQL code to another server, the database engine (JET on NT) to perform the database query. JET passes the results back to the ColdFusion server, which reformats the results based on descriptions in the template into HTML. These results are sent back to the user. Figure 3.3 shows these steps.

Our new page performs two functions when it is viewed:

- To update the AccessLog database with information about this access. Users will not be aware of this unless they are told.
- To count the number of records in the database's table and send that number back to the user. The user is never aware of this activity either, other than seeing the result as a number.

The new code, this time saved as a *.cfm* file is as follows:

```
<HTML>
<TITLE>My Web Page</TITLE>
<BODY>
<CFQUERY datasource="MyLog" name="Hits">
      Select        *
```

```
	from Log
</CFQUERY>
<CENTER>
<H1>My Web Page</H1>
<P>Welcome to my page, glad you could come!
<P>Here is what I look like: <BR><BR>
<IMG src="mugshot.jpg">
<P>You are the
<CFOUTPUT>
#Hits.Recordcount#
</CFOUTPUT>
 visitor to this site.</P>
</CENTER>
</BODY>
</HTML>
```

The <CFQUERY> tag

There are two differences between this code and the normal HTML code that we described earlier. The first is the CF Query tag:

```
<CFQUERY datasource="MyLog" name="Hits">
	Select	*
	from Log
</CFQUERY>
```

This command is one of the most common that is used when accessing a database. It runs the SQL statement inside the tag on the database table *Log* which is accessed via the ODBC datasource called *MyLog*. A datasource is a link to a database (or some other form of data) on the computer or server. The name is the method that the template uses to refer to this query later on. Several queries can be run in the same template, so there needs to be a way of differentiating them.

The SQL statement means, *get all of the records and fields from the table called Log.* It does not actually do anything with them at the moment, just holds them in memory on the server for later use. These records can then be sent to the HTML document using the <CFOUTPUT> tag. The <CFQUERY> is also given a name, in this case *Hits* which is used to refer to this data later on in the template file.

The <CFOUTPUT> Tag

The only other change to the file is where the actual number of page requests is reported to the user. This is done with the following code:

```
<CFOUTPUT>
    #Hits.Recordcount#
</CFOUTPUT>
```

The <CFOUTPUT> tag, alerts ColdFusion to the fact that it has to do something with the text inside the tag. The hashes signify that the code inside them is a reference to a ColdFusion variable or function. In this case **Hits** is the query that we want to find the amount of records that have been logged, and **.Recordcount** counts the number of records in the **Hits** query and returns them as a number.

Viewing the Results

When this code is resident on a server and a user requests the page, the user is not aware of any of the ColdFusion code that had been run. In fact, if the user views the code, (by for instance selecting **View Source** from the **View** menu in Internet Explorer) the following code would appear:

```
<HTML>
<TITLE>My Web Page</TITLE>
<BODY>
<CENTER>
<H1>My Web Page</H1>
<P>Welcome to my page, glad you could come!
<P>Here is what I look like: <BR><BR>
<IMG src="mugshot.jpg">
```

```
<P>You are the 216 visitor to this site.</P>
</CENTER>
</BODY>
</HTML>
```

Notice the ColdFusion tags that were in the template file do not appear in the final code that the user's browser views. Also notice that the output from the <CFOUTPUT> tag is just a number. To the user, it appears as if this HTML code has been written personally for them. The user is unaware that a database retrieval has been performed when they looked at the page. The only possible clue that this is a not a standard HTML file is that the file extension *.cfm* may be seen in the browser's location window.

Using <CFQUERY>

The template file above is incomplete as a working page counter, since although it includes the code to count the number of records or page hits in the database, there is no method to log each page request to the database. Currently if we refreshed or reloaded this page the number of hits would never rise since we are not incrementing it. To generate a page 'hit' we have to add the following code to the template:

```
<CFQUERY name="addhit" datasource="MyLog">
Insert into Log (AccessDateAndTime,PageName,HostIPNum)
Values (#Now()#,'HomePage','#CGI.REMOTE_HOST#')
</CFQUERY>
```

This code creates a new record in the database with the values supplied in the SQL statement. Notice that inside the first set of brackets are the field names of the **Log** table we planned in figure 3.2, to which the Microsoft Access design implementation is shown in figure 3.4. Only a few fields are used here, and as long as you do not specify any fields as mandatory when you are creating your datasource, you can use as few or as many fields here as required. For now we will use just three. Three values have to be inserted under the corresponding field names.

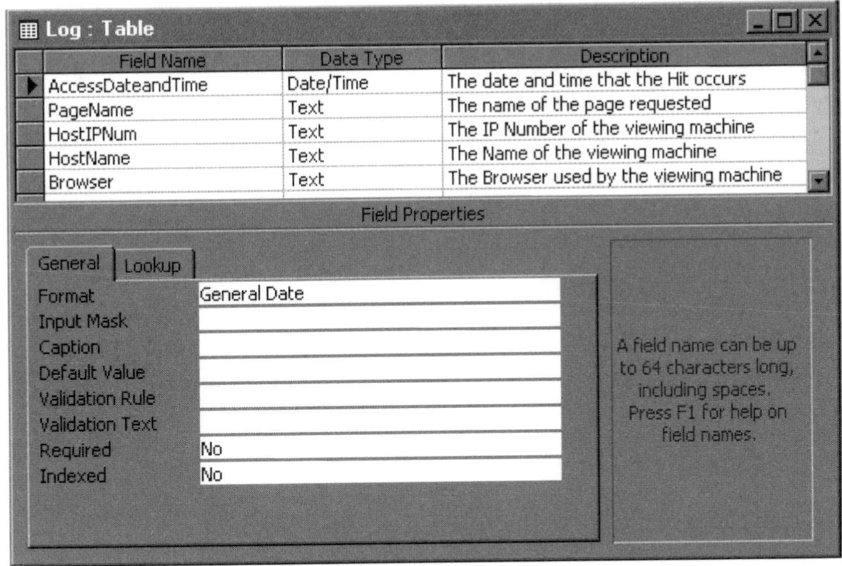

Figure 3.4 – The Log table as implemented in Microsoft Access.

The **Now()** function is a ColdFusion function that takes the server's system time and date and converts it into the correct format to be included as a date field in the table. Depending on how you designed the table different formats may be required for this statement. More information about ColdFusion functions is given in chapter 11.

Homepage is a string that describes the name of the page that was viewed. Currently this is redundant, as our system comprises of only one page, but later on we could add the access log code to other pages, so it is useful to log which page is being viewed at this point.

The hashes around *#CGI.REMOTE_ADDR#* signify that it is a ColdFusion variable. In this case it makes reference to one of the CGI variables which are available to scripts running on the web server. This particular variable stores the unique machine number, or IP number, that every machine accessing the Internet must have. Depending on what web server you are using it may return the DNS name of the machine instead. As it may return a number or a string, we store it as a string in our table. We can add this anywhere within our HTML file, and the user will not be aware of its presence. The ColdFusion server runs it, acquires the data and puts it as a record into the database.

So our final working page counter code is:

```
<HTML>
<TITLE>My Web Page</TITLE>
<BODY>
<CFQUERY datasource="MyLog" name="Hits">
	Select	*
	from Log
</CFQUERY>
<CENTER>
<H1>My Web Page</H1>
<P>Welcome to my page, glad you could come!
<P>Here is what I look like: <BR><BR>
<IMG src="mugshot.jpg">
<P>You are the
<CFOUTPUT>
#Hits.Recordcount#
</CFOUTPUT>
 visitor to this site.</P>
</CENTER>
<CFQUERY name="addhit" datasource="MyLog">
Insert into Log (AccessDateAndTime,PageName,HostIPNum)
Values (#Now()#,'HomePage','#CGI.REMOTE_HOST#')
</CFQUERY>
</BODY>
</HTML>
```

Every time the user views the page, a new record is generated, storing the time and their details. At the same time, the server retrieves all of these records, counts them and returns the count back to the user as the page hit count. The page when rendered in a browser will look similar to the original one shown in figure 3.1.

Viewing visitor logs

So far we have been able to store some information about the users of our web pages, but have not got much information back. Ideally we do not want to share all of our information with a normal user of our pages. To prevent this we will create a separate web page that lists the contents of our database. We need to create a new template file, which we will call *log.cfm*.

We start with a standard HTML file as normal, which we save with the above filename. A standard file is shown below:

```
<HTML>
<TITLE>My web page access log</TITLE>
<BODY>
<P>This page lists the accesses to my pages. (Apart from this one)
</BODY>
</HTML>
```

To gain access to the log table we can use the same query we used previously, that is:

```
<CFQUERY datasource="MyLog" name="HitList">
      Select      *
      from Log
</CFQUERY>
```

However, in this example we are only going to list the date and time and the IP number or DNS name of each record, so the SQL statement changes to:

```
Select HostIPNum,AccessDateAndTime
from Log
```

It does not have to change, you can still use the * to retrieve all fields, but it speeds things slightly if you only ask for what you want to use or view.

If we added this code into the *log.cfm* file, when the file is viewed it will not show any results: therefore we have to use the <CFOUTPUT> tag in a slightly more complex way than the last way we used it. The following code can be added to the file:

```
<CFOUTPUT query="HitList">
#AccessDateandTime#-#HostIPNum#<BR>
</CFOUTPUT>
```

This code outputs database records to the browser. The query attribute within the tag refers to the name of the <CFQUERY> tag that the system will be outputting.

Then, in this example, the code that follows will be output for every record in the table:

- The date and time of the access.
- a hyphen.
- the IP number of the accessing machine.
- A <BR> tag, from standard HTML, moves to the next line of the screen so that each record starts on a new line and the results are more readable.

The output from this code is shown in figure 3.5:

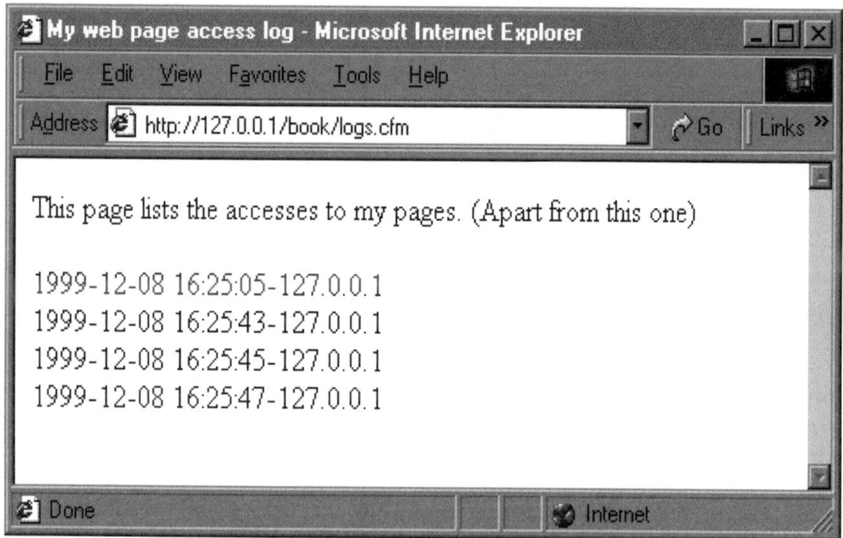

***Figure 3.5** – Basic text based output.*

As our web pages get more hits, this page will get larger. If we only want to look at a few records we can reduce the amount of data that comes back to the viewer by adding the **maxrows** attribute to the <CFOUTPUT> tag:

```
<CFOUTPUT query="Hits" maxrows=10>
```

This will limit the maximum number of records output to 10. The **maxrows** attribute can be used in the <CFQUERY> tag in a similar fashion.

Formatting the output

In our example of a query output, as the number of rows increases, we see how all of the numbers begin to become difficult to read especially when the columns do not line up correctly. We can resolve this problem by putting the text into a table, rather than a simple text string which we do by replacing the previous <CFOUTPUT> as follows:

```
<TABLE border =1>
<CFOUTPUT query="HitList" maxrows=10>
 <TR>
       <TD>#AccessDateandTime#</TD>
       <TD>#HostIPNum#</TD>
</TR>
</CFOUTPUT>
</TABLE>
```

Figure 3.6 shows what this is like when it is rendered. To complete the page it would be useful to add the field names to the top of the table identifying the columns. This can be done by adding an extra row before the <CFOUTPUT> and after the <TABLE> tags:

```
<TR><TD>Access Time</TD> <TD>Host IP Number</TD></TR>
```

This code adds an extra row containing the headings to the table, which is added before ColdFusion starts looping through the records.

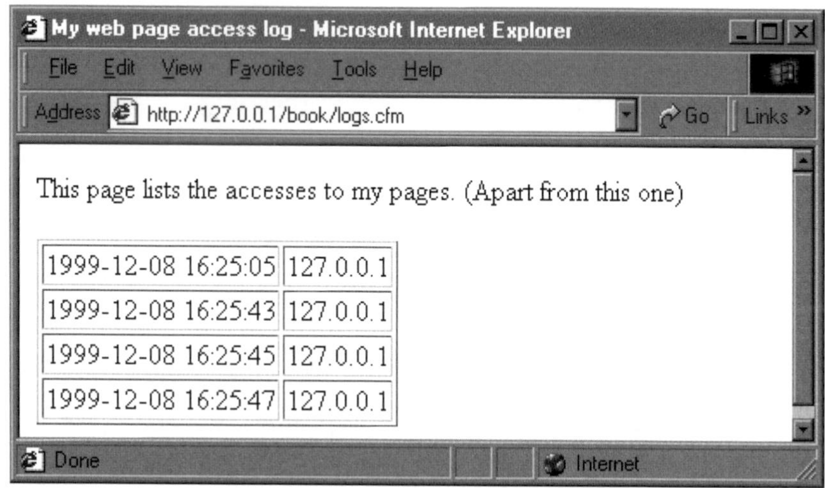

***Figure 3.6** – Tabular output of database.*

Our final code to list the database hits is as follows:

```
<HTML>
<TITLE>My web page access log</TITLE>
<CFQUERY datasource="MyLog" name="HitList">
	Select	HostIPNum,AccessDateAndTime
	from Log
</CFQUERY>
<BODY>
<P>This page lists the accesses to my pages. (Apart from this one)
<P>
<TABLE border =1>
<TR><TD>Access Time</TD> <TD>Host IP Number</TD></TR>
<CFOUTPUT query="HitList" maxrows=10>
 <TR>
	<TD>#AccessDateandTime#</TD>
	<TD>#HostIPNum#</TD>
</TR>
</CFOUTPUT>
</TABLE>
Total Hits : <CFOUTPUT>#HitList.Recordcount#</CFOUTPUT>
</BODY>
</HTML>
```

This code has the record count added at the end to give us the total number of hits as an extra statistic. The final rendered output is shown in figure 3.7.

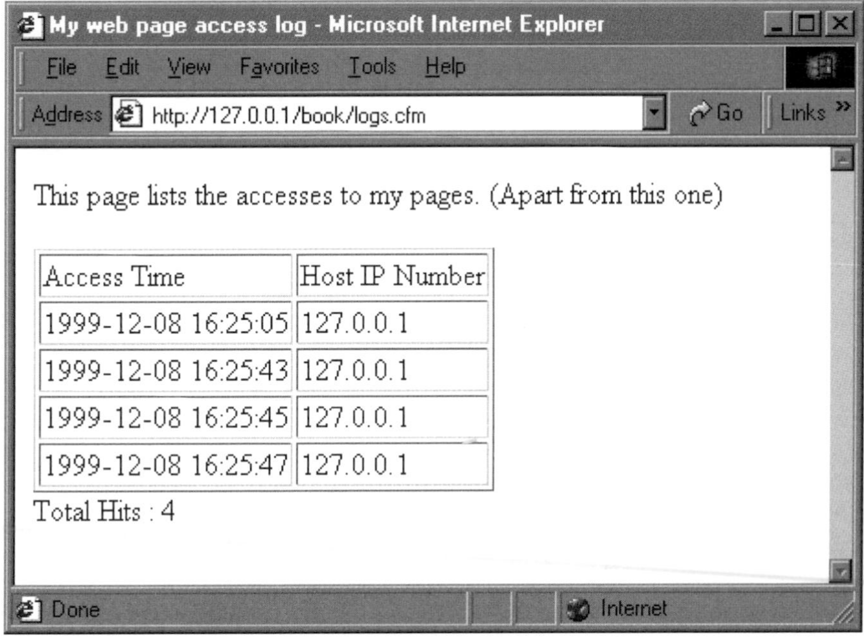

***Figure 3.7** – Final output of database list.*

In this chapter we have looked at a useful ColdFusion application for logging and counting the accesses to a web page.

Now that you have been introduced to the concepts behind a ColdFusion application and setting up a system to develop ColdFusion on, we briefly review the use of HTML before we start coding properly in ColdFusion.

Chapter 4

HTML for ColdFusion

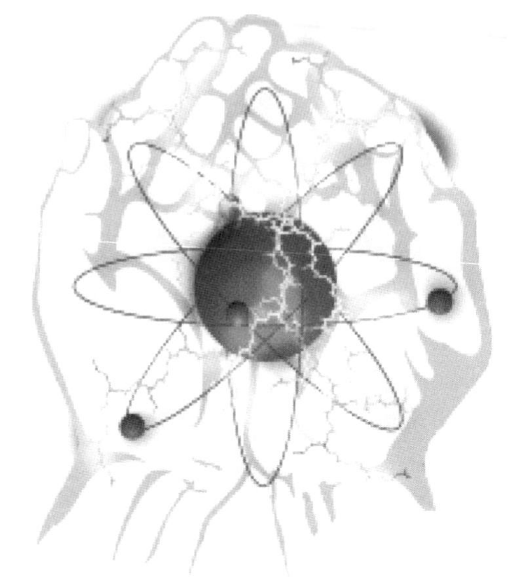

Introduction

All web pages are created using HTML, or Hyper Text Markup Language. The HTML consists of a series of tags saved in a text file. The browser will read through the tags and format the text depending on the commands in the tags.

A tag consists of a word or letters inside the less than and greater than sign as follows:

```
<TAG>
```

A tag works on its own, which triggers a single action, or with an end tag, which then applies the command in the tag to everything between the start and end tag:

```
<TAG>  other text or tags </TAG>
```

A tag can also contain a set of attributes, which affect the functioning of the tag. Each attribute can be a single statement, or a statement attached to a value as follows:

```
<TAG attribute1="Attribute value" attribute2>
```

The <HTML> tag

Every HTML document has the basic framework of tags as follows:

```
<HTML>
<HEAD>
</HEAD>
<BODY>
</BODY>
</HTML>
```

The <HTML> tag defines the start and end of the HTML code. The **HEAD** section of the HTML code contains information about the page, and certain control and information fields. The **BODY** section contains the actual contents of the page to be displayed.

Naming the title bar with<TITLE>

The most commonly used tag in the header section is the <TITLE> tag. The title tag puts whatever you put inside of it into the Title box on your browser, for example the following HTML produces the title bar shown in figure 4.1.

```
<HTML>
<HEAD>
<TITLE>An empty web page</TITLE>
</HEAD>
<BODY>
</BODY>
</HTML>
```

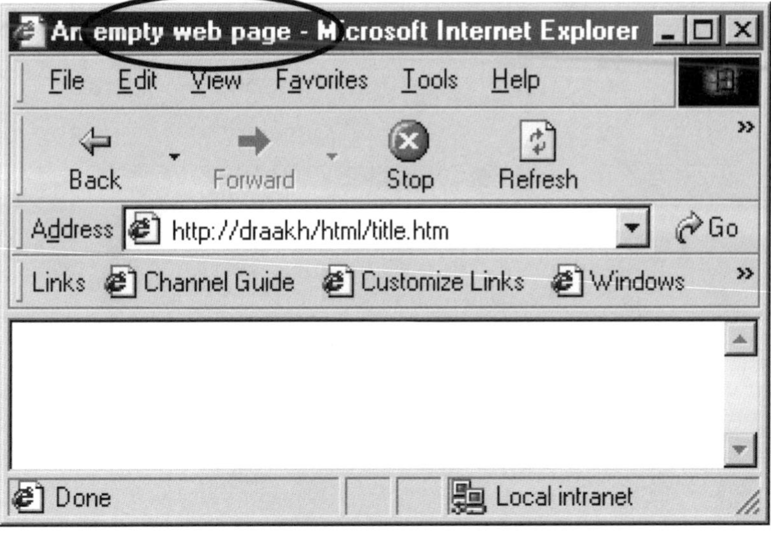

***Figure 4.1** – The Title bar.*

The Paragraph tag <P>

The browser will work along your HTML code in the BODY of the document sequentially, ignoring multiple spaces or carriage returns. So as to begin to format your text you can use the paragraph tag <P> to make your text go to the next line and leave a space as a paragraph does. The following extreme example shows this in figure 4.2:

```
<HTML>
<HEAD>
<TITLE>Paragraph tag</TITLE>
</HEAD>
<BODY>
<P>The most commonly used tag in the header section is the TITLE tag. The title tag
puts whatever you put inside of it into the Title box on your browser, for example the
following HTML<P>The browser will work along your HTML code sequentially,
ignoring any spaces or carriage returns. To begin to format your text you can use the
paragraph tag to make your text go to the next line and leave a space as a paragraph
does. The following extreme example shows this
</BODY>
</HTML>
```

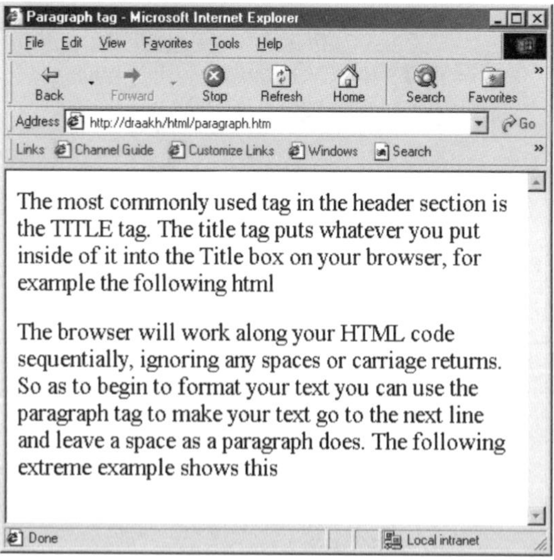

Figure 4.2 – Using the paragraph <P> tag.

Depending on the size of your browser window the above HTML will format your text into recognizable paragraphs on the web page as shown in figure 4.2.

The Line Break tag

Sometimes you may want to fix the width of the lines on the screen. You can force line breaks by using the <BR> tag.

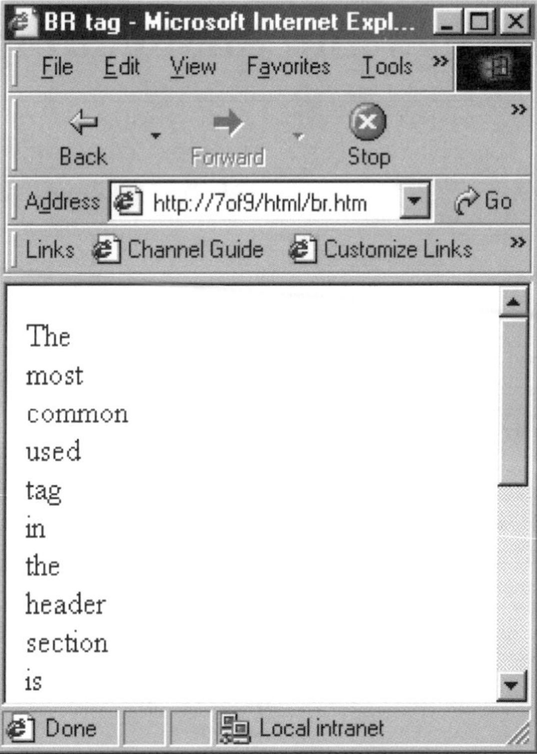

Figure 4.3 *– The Break <BR> tag.*

Figure 4.3 shows another extreme example created with the following code.

```
<HTML>
<HEAD>
<TITLE>Paragraph tag</TITLE>
</HEAD>
<BODY>
<P>The<BR>most <BR>commonly <BR>used<BR> tag<BR> in<BR> the<BR>
header<BR> section<BR> is<BR> the <TITLE> tag<BR>. The<BR> title<BR> tag
puts<BR> whatever<BR> you <BR>put<BR> inside<BR> of<BR> it<BR>
</BODY>
</HTML>
```

Headings and Subheadings <H1>

There are several built-in ways of formatting text using the Heading tags. The most commonly used are <H1> to <H4>. Figure 4.4 shows the following HTML demonstrating these:

```
<HTML>
<HEAD>
	<TITLE>Text Formatting</TITLE>
</HEAD>
<BODY>
<H1>Heading Level 1</H1>
<H2>Heading Level 2</H2>
<H3>Heading Level 3</H3>
<P>There are several built in methods of formatting text called
the Heading tags. You can also use the<B> bold</B> and the
<I >italic</I> tags to format text within a paragraph.
</BODY>
</HTML>
```

Bold and Italics

You can also use the bold <B> and the italic <I> tags to format text within a paragraph. The use of these tags is shown in the above code and Figure 4.4.

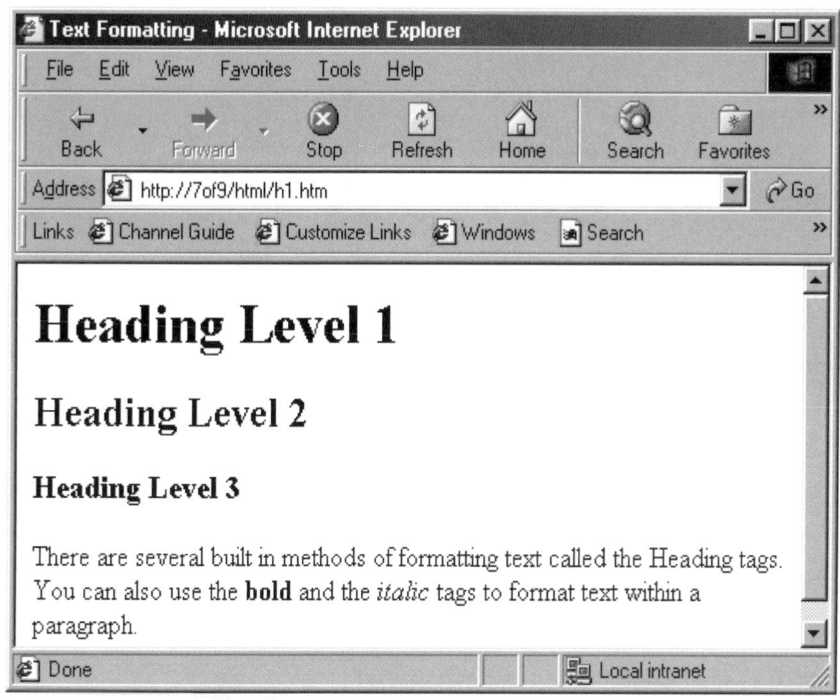

Figure 4.4 – Simple text formatting.

Inserting a picture <IMG>

To insert an image in a document you use the image tag <IMG>. Basic use of the tag contains an attribute called *src*, which points to the location and name of the image file. You use a Dos convention to point to the files, that is if you do not provide a path name the Image is assumed to be in the same directory as the calling HTML file. You can, however, include an image from anywhere on the Internet by putting the full URL of the image into the source attribute, as long as you remember to put *http://* in front of the URL. You can also use the width and height attribute to stretch, shrink and distort the image in pixels. Figure 4.5 shows several links to the same image as created in the following HTML. Notice in the figure how the browser copes with images that are not available as in the second image.

```
<HTML>
<HEAD>
	<TITLE>Images</TITLE>
</HEAD>
<BODY>
<IMG src="mugshot.jpg">
<IMG src="Nofile">
<IMG src="mugshot.jpg" width=20>
<IMG src="mugshot.jpg" width=20 height=100>
</BODY>
</HTML>
```

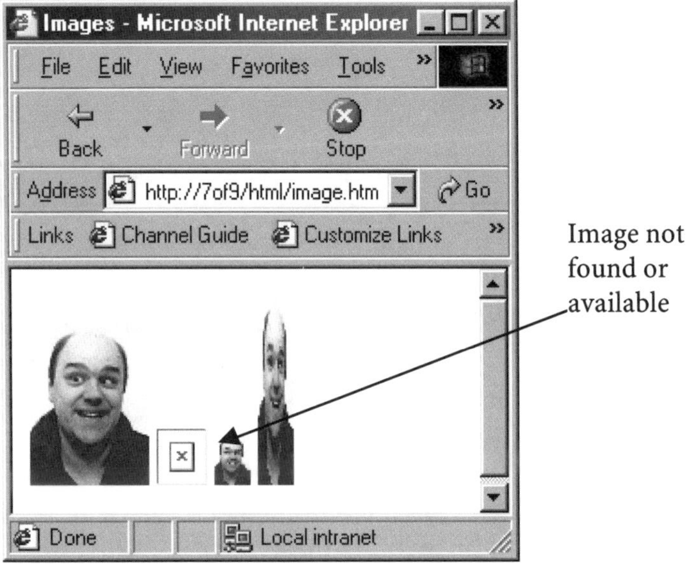

Figure 4.5 – <IMG> tag resizing images.

Adding a link with <A>

To put a link onto another page, you use the anchor tab <A>. This tag has an attribute called **href**, which is the address or name of the file to display when the link is followed. The **href** works in a similar way to the **src** attribute of image, in that it can refer to file in the same directory or files elsewhere on the Internet. The anchor tag turns whatever it encloses into a link. This can include images as well as text.

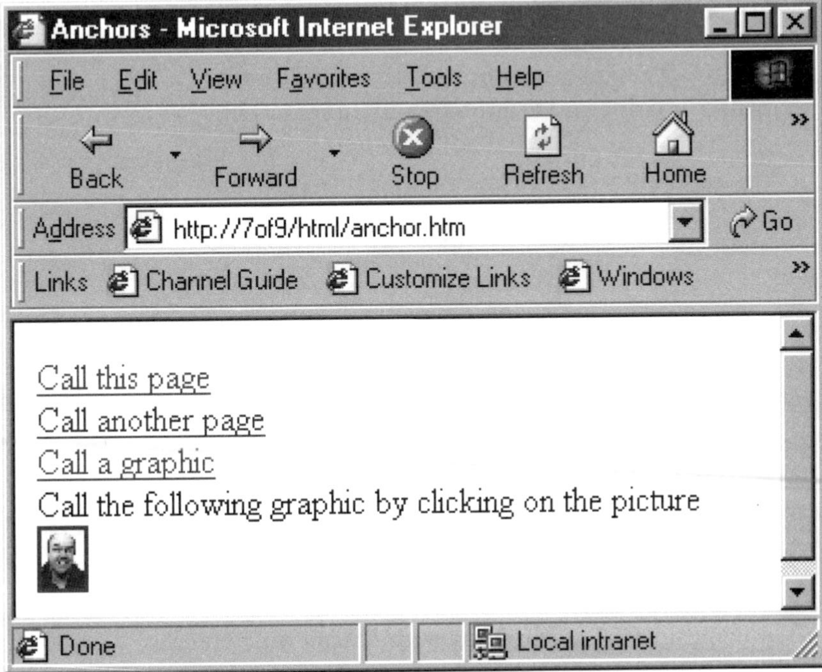

***Figure 4.6** – Different uses of the anchor tag.*

Figure 4.6 shows the anchor being used to call a link, as well as a bigger version of the image that is linked. The following HTML accomplishes this:

```
<HTML>
<HEAD>
    <TITLE>Anchors</TITLE>
</HEAD>
<BODY>
    <A href="anchor.htm">Call this page</A><BR>
    <A href="http://www.easyrew.com?ecf">Call another page</A><BR>
    <A href="mugshot.jpg">Call a graphic</A><BR>
```

```
    Call the following graphic by clicking on the picture<BR>
    <A href="mugshot.jpg"><IMG src="mugshot.jpg" width=20></A>
</BODY>
</HTML>
```

The <TABLE> Feature

Further layout on the web page can be accomplished by means of the <TABLE> functions. The <TABLE> tag uses two more tags to control layout, that of the table row tag <TR> and the table data tag <TD>.

- *<TABLE>* defines the individual table.
- *<TR>* defines the particular row we are dealing with, there can be many and they all must fit within a table tag.
- *<TD>* defines an individual cell of data within the table row.

The following HTML document shows how all of these tags work together. It is probably best that you do not try typing it all in as it probably isn't worth the effort! Have a look on the website or just look at figure 4.7.

```
<HTML>
<HEAD>
    <TITLE>Table</TITLE>
</HEAD>
<BODY>
<H1>March</H1>
<TABLE>
<TR><td>Mon</td><td>Tues</td><td>Wed</td><td>Thur</td><td>Fri</td><td>S
at</td><td>Sun</td></TR>
<TR><td></td><td></td><td>1</td><td>2</td><td>3</td><td>4</td><td>5</td
></TR>
<TR><td>6</td><td>7</td><td>8</td><td>9</td><td>10</td><td>11</td><td>1
2</td></TR>
<TR><td>13</td><td>14</td><td>15</td><td>16</td><td>17</td><td>18</td><
td>19</td></TR>
<TR><td>20</td><td>21</td><td>22</td><td>23</td><td>24</td><td>25</td><
td>26</td></TR>
```

```
<TR><td>27</td><td>28</td><td>29</td><td>30</td><td>31</td><td></td><td
></td></TR>
</table>
</BODY>
</HTML>
```

This looks really complex until you realise what it is doing. The table has 6 rows, each with 7 cells. The first is the title row which contains the days of the week. The following 5 rows have 7 cells: each one has the date in it or is left blank. The output of this is shown in figure 4.7.

***Figure 4.7** – <TABLE> tags used to create a calendar.*

Tables are a great way to lay out your page without using frames. You can use various attributes to set the alignment of the contents of the cells, as well as the colours and backgrounds. Do not think that the only use of the table is to output numerical, spreadsheet-style data. Tables are a powerful way of creatively laying out your pages. When designing your pages using tables it is best to use the **border=1** attribute in the table tag to check the layout.

The horizontal rule <HR> tag

While the table tag can be used to draw lines there is a simple way of dividing the screen with a line by using the horizontal rule tag <HR>. This tag is inserted anywhere you want a line and does not require a close tag. <HR> is very useful for dividing many records that have been output on a single web page as can be seen in chapter 6 in figure 6.2.

Acquiring user input <FORM>

The <FORM> tag is used to pass data to another page. This data can be read by any type of web-based scripting languages. An HTML file that contains a form can call another HTML file but the called file cannot access the form fields unless it is being processed by some server-based code.

The form has an action tag and a method tag, the first contains the name of the page that the form calls and the latter contains the method that the form uses to send its contents.

The following HTML sets up a form with most of the common form controls. Every form control has a name, which the receiving page uses like a variable to obtain the form data in that specified field.

```
<HTML>
<HEAD>
	<TITLE>Form example</TITLE>
</HEAD>
<BODY>
<FORM action="nextpage.cfm" method="post">
<BR>Text Field: <INPUT type="Text" value="Text field, type here" name="TextField">
<BR>Password Field: <INPUT type="Password" name="password1">
```

```
<BR>Hidden field: <INPUT type="Hidden" value="Secret! Wont appear"
name="secret">
<BR>Checkbox:
<BR><INPUT type="Checkbox" name="check" value="option1"> value1
<BR><INPUT type="Checkbox" name="check" value="option2"> value2
<BR><INPUT type="Checkbox" name="check" value="option3"> value3
<BR>Radio Buttons:
<BR><INPUT type="Radio" name="radio" value="option1"> value1
<BR><INPUT type="Radio" name="radio" value="option2"> value2
<BR><INPUT type="Radio" name="radio" value="option3"> value3
<BR><INPUT type="Submit" value="Send Form Data">
</form>
</BODY>
</HTML>
```

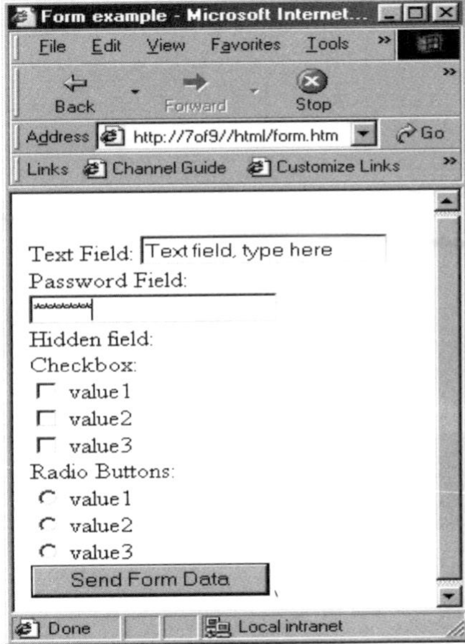

***Figure 4.8** – Example form controls.*

Figure 4.8 shows this file when rendered in a browser. Each of the inputs has various functions. The checkbox input will return a list of values for each one that is ticked. The radio button will only allow one value to be passed through to the next web page.

This chapter gives a quick introduction to HTML and should be sufficient to use and understand most of the examples in this book. This chapter has not described all of the subtleties of HTML and I encourage you to go and find out about the rest. The thing to remember is that HTML is essentially a very simple, readable code stored in text documents. Although designing an interesting, efficient web page is still not easy, you can type the HTML required in an application as simple as Notepad.

HTML is not a hard language to master. Learn it by example. If you wonder how a web page you find is made then view the source code with your browser. Most of the time you can read through it and see how it is done. You can even cut and paste HTML code that you find into your own HTML files and customize it. Most word processors now even allow you to save your document as HTML.

Chapter

5

Using SQL

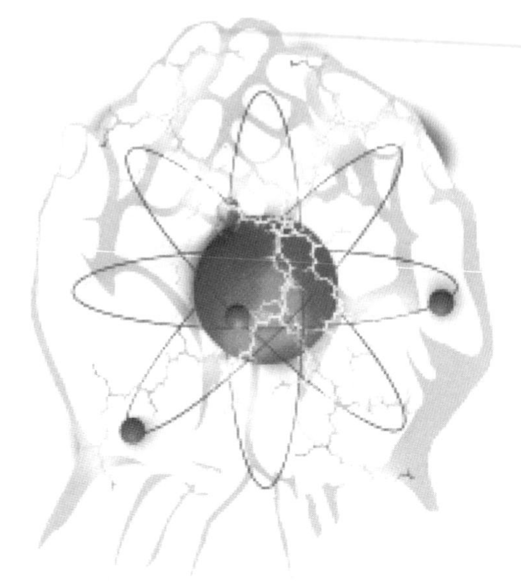

Introduction

SQL (or Structured Query Language) is a method of interrogating databases by means of textual commands. The language itself comprises a small number of commands which can be put together quickly to produce amazingly complex searches. If you are going to use the full power of ColdFusion you will not be able to escape using SQL.

To illustrate various commands described in this chapter we will use the datasource described earlier however, we will leave our access log table alone. Then we create a new table for our SQL testing within the datasource, and then interrogate and add to it using only SQL statements and the ColdFusion Server.

SQL's command set

Some of the commands available to you as an SQL user, and useful to you as a ColdFusion developer are as follows:

- CREATE TABLE.
- SELECT.
- UPDATE.
- INSERT.
- DELETE.

Each command will have a series of parameters, and will end with a semicolon (;). You can format the SQL as you like, using spaces and carriage returns, to make it look neater or more understandable. The SQL interpreter will just work along a line ignoring these until it gets to a semicolon.

SQL data types

A data type is a definition of how a database stores its data. For example, a number from 1 to 10 may be stored differently to an address, a telephone number or a graphic. So SQL has a set of pre-defined data types that you can use to store your data efficiently. Some of these are:

- **char(x)** – A string of alphanumeric characters of fixed length (x characters)
- **varchar(x)** – A string of alphanumeric characters of variable length not exceeding x characters.
- **Integer** – A number, within a preset range. The range depends on the systems. For example a number between –32768 and 32768
- **Boolean** – A binary value, that can be either 1 or 0. It is also represented as True or False, and Yes or No.
- **date/time** – A method of storing the date and time.

When creating a table the data type of each column has to be predefined. However when using an ODBC datasource, the data types are dependent on the underlying database when creating and updating tables. So if we use SQL server as our back-end data server the data types above are correct, but in our example system so far, we are using Microsoft Access to create the datasources. This means that the data types will be the same as you would use within Access to define tables. So to compare the data types in SQL and in Access refer to table 5.1:

Table 5.1 – Data types in SQL and Access.

SQL	Access
char	Text
varchar	Text
integer	Number
boolean	Yes/No
date/time	Date/Time

In this chapter we will create a table inside our datasource to act as a visitors' book for the site. This application allows a visitor to add a comment or message to the web site if they wish. It will store the following data:

- Name.
- Email.
- Comment.
- Date and Time.
- Where the user is.
- Did they like the site.

A decision needs to be made of how to store our visitor book data. As noted earlier, we are using Access so need to use Access data types. Most of the fields are the datatype **Text**, however the *Date and Time* will be the **Date/Time** type, and the *Did they like the site* will be a **Yes/No** datatype. So we can represent our table as follows:

VisitorBook
Name Email Comment DateAndTime Location LikeSite?

Figure 5.1 *– Visitor book data structure.*

Now we have designed our data structure we will briefly look at how to go about creating it in SQL. In practice, however, it would be easier to use Access to create the table.

CREATE TABLE

This command allows the creation of a new table in the datasource. To use the command you need a table name and a list of fields, along with the type of data that will be used in each field.

The CREATE TABLE command has the following basic format:

```
CREATE TABLE tablename
( columnname datatype , more columnnames..... );
```

Therefore to create our new table, VisitorBook, we need the following SQL command:

```
CREATE TABLE VisitorBook
(Name text,
 Email text,
Comment text,
DateAndTime Date/time,
Location text,
LikeSite Yes/No );
```

We will now go through the steps involved in creating the above table in Access. Start Access and load in your datasource, which if you have followed previous chapters will be in:

```
c:\Inetpub\odbc\accesslog.mdb
```

You will now see your existing table, Log displayed as in figure 5.2. We create a new table as follows:

- Click on the **New** button as shown and when it asks how you wish to create a table select **design view** and click on **OK**. You will be presented with a dialog similar to figure 5.3.

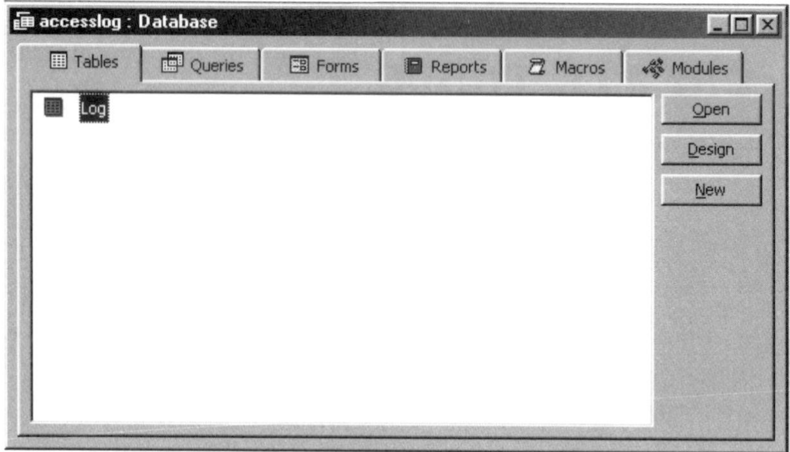

Figure 5.2 – The existing Log table.

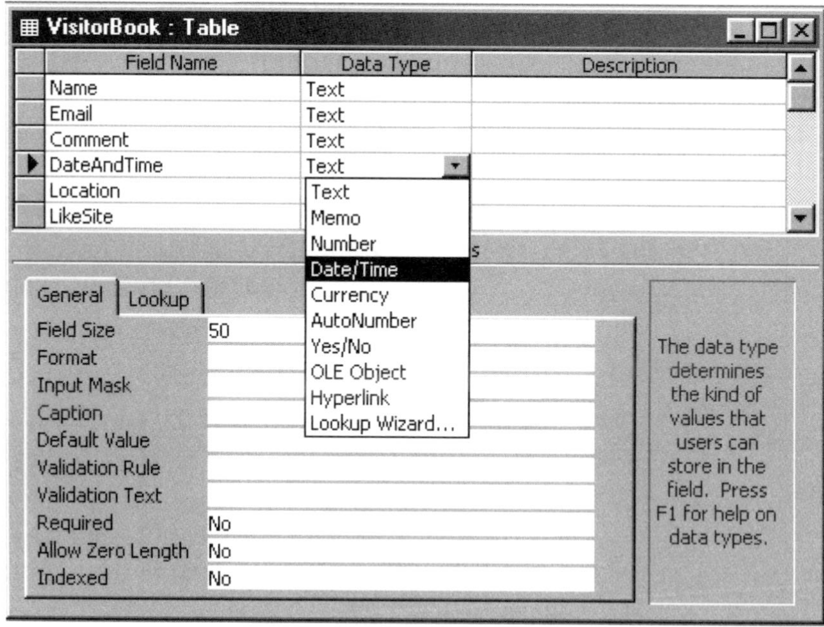

Figure 5.3 – Creating the new table.

- Type in the field names as in figure 5.3. Each time you press return the data type will default to *Text*.

- When you get to the **DateAndTime** field click into the **Data Type** cell that follows it and click on the small triangle. You will be presented with a drop down box as shown in the figure.
- Select the **Date/Time** type. Continue typing until you get to *LikeSite* and do the same, but this time select the **Yes/No** type.
- Click on the floppy disk icon on the button bar to save the table, and when it prompts you for a name type *VisitorBook.*
- If Access asks you if you want to create a primary key just click **Yes.** The primary key is a unique field in a table which becomes the primary reference to that record. Access will add another field to the table called *ID* which we will use later to reference a specific entry in our visitor book. This field will be given a unique number every time a new record is created. We can immediately refer back to this record by using this key.

You will now have two tables in your database as shown in figure 5.4.

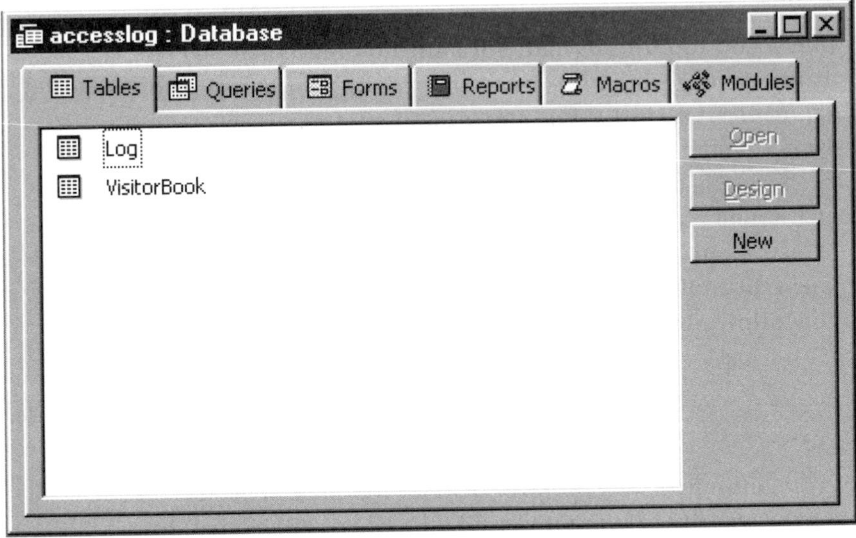

***Figure 5.4** – The new table VisitorBook.*

INSERT

We now need to add some data into the table, which uses the SQL command INSERT. This command takes the following format in SQL:

```
INSERT into TABLENAME (FieldName1,FieldName2, ....)
VALUES (Data1,Data2,.....);
```

The INSERT command adds a new record to the table putting the data given into the fields specified. All fields in the table do not have to be specified; however, all that are must have corresponding data of the correct type in the values list. So to insert data into our visitors' book would require an INSERT statement as follows:

```
INSERT INTO VisitorBook(Name, Email, DateandTime, Comment)
VALUES ('Simon Marsh','simon@nowhere.com',#Now()#,'Awful site mate');
```

We will leave the **Yes/No** field for the moment as it is a special case. Notice how in the VALUES clause each field that has a **text** data type has quotes around it. The date and time, however, do not. **Now()**, is a ColdFusion function that creates a date object that the database engine can recognize. Now we have the syntax of the SQL it needs to be sent to the database engine which is done by wrapping it in a <CFQUERY> as follows:

```
<CFQUERY name="TestInsert" datasource="MyLog">
    INSERT INTO VisitorBook(Name, Email, DateandTime, Comment)
    VALUES ('Simon Marsh','simon@nowhere.com',
        #Now()#,'Awful site mate')
</CFQUERY>
```

Inside the <CFQUERY> tag there are two parameters:

- **Name** identifies the query so that it can be referred to later on in the template as needed.
- **Datasource** identifies the datasource on the server that this SQL statement is to be run on. Notice also how it does not matter where you put spaces and returns: unless they are in the middle of quotes they

are ignored, the database engine moves along the text from left to right and top to bottom.

To test this query it needs to be inserted into a *.cfm* template file and saved somewhere in the *wwwroot* of your web server. Create a directory on your web server inside the *wwwroot* directory called *sql*. We will put all of the test files for this chapter in there. In each case we will need to insert our queries into a *.cfm* template file. For this chapter we will use the following as a base document each time:

```
<HTML>
<TITLE>SQL TEST FILE</TITLE>
<BODY>
  <!--- insert code here --->
</BODY>
<HTML>
```

For example we take our previous <CFQUERY> and insert it into the above template to give us the following file:

```
<HTML>
<TITLE>SQL TEST FILE</TITLE>
<BODY>
  <CFQUERY name="TestInsert" datasource="MyLog">
      INSERT INTO VisitorBook(Name, Email, DateandTime, Comment)
      VALUES ('Simon Marsh','simon@nowhere.com',
             #Now()#,'Awful site mate')
      </CFQUERY>
</BODY>
<HTML>
```

Type the above into a text editor and save it in your web server's *wwwroot\sql* directory calling it *inserttest.cfm*. The application is now ready for testing. Start up a web browser and type in the following address:

```
http://WebServerName/sql/inserttest.cfm
```

WebServerName is the name of your computer running ColdFusion and the web server. You should be rewarded with a blank browser page as in figure 5.5; the page correctly contains nothing, again proving that ColdFusion can be doing much behind the scenes without showing anything obvious to the user. If, for some reason, ColdFusion generates an error, check your typing for errors. To really test what has gone on behind the scenes open up your datasource in access and view the *VisitorBook* table. It should look something like figure 5.6.

Figure 5.5 *– The Insert statement's 'output'.*

VisitorBook : Table

	Name	Email	Comment	DateAndTime	Location	LikeSite	ID
▶	Simon Marsh	simon@nowher	Awful site mate	/06/00 21:53:47		☐	1
*						☐	(AutoNumber)

Record: 1 of 1

Figure 5.6 *– The inserted data.*

You will see that the database engine has left blank every field that was not provided in the insert list, with the exception of the ID which is the field that Access created as a primary key. This field had the data type AutoNumber, which the database engine will automatically increment for each new record. This is a useful way of referring to the record later. Close the table and exit Access. Open up your *inserttest.cfm* and alter some of the data to different names. Save the file again and reload the file using the web browser several times. Change the name again and repeat this process to build up at least five records that we can use in the later examples. Open up the datasource again and check the new records are there and notice the differences between them.

SELECT

Now we have some data to work with we will begin to bring some of that data back with the SQL **SELECT** command. The format of this command is:

```
SELECT     FieldNames
FROM       TableName
[WHERE condition]
[ORDER BY FieldName ASC/DESC]
```

FieldNames are fields within the table *TableName* separated by commas. There is a special case where you can use an asterisk as the *FieldName*, which selects all fields from the table. The *Where* clause is used to select specific records that match the condition. This can be omitted which is what we shall do at this time, as can the **ORDER BY** which will be discussed later. So to select all of the records from our VisitorBook Table, in a CFQUERY, we use the following code:

```
<CFQUERY name="SelectAll" datasource="MyLog">
    SELECT    *
    FROM      VisitorBook
</CFQUERY>
```

Insert the above code into a base document described earlier and save it in your *sql* directory on the web server as *selectall.cfm*. Before we can test this we need to provide some method of outputting the data from the query. We do this using the <CFOUTPUT> tag and the record names as variables as follows:

```
<CFOUTPUT query="SelectAll">
	#Name#<BR>
	#Email#<BR>
	#DateAndTime#<BR>
	#Comment#<BR>
	#LikeSite#<BR>
	#ID#<BR>
	<BR>
</CFOUTPUT>
```

Type the above into your *selectall.cfm* file after the <CFQUERY> section. The <CFOUTPUT> takes the data obtained from the *SelectAll* query and will loop through the code inside the <CFOUTPUT> tag once for each record returned by the query. So inside this tag we have the hashes to signify that what is inside the hashes are tokens to be evaluated by ColdFusion (in this instance field names) and
s which just makes sure that each field starts on a new line, with a blank line between records. Save the file again and point your web browser at it again by typing:

```
http://WebServerName/sql/selectall.cfm
```

into the Address box of the browser. Figure 5.7 gives a section of the page returned from the author's data, yours will look different depending on what you typed inside the INSERT statements in the previous section.

You will see from figure 5.7 that the ID field is successfully incrementing each time, and that so far five records have been inserted into the database.

We will now alter the SQL statement to make it more specific and concise by only selecting the fields that we are going to use. Load in your *selectall.cfm* file and edit the SQL statement so that it reads as follows:

```
SELECT	ID,Name
FROM	VisitorBook
```

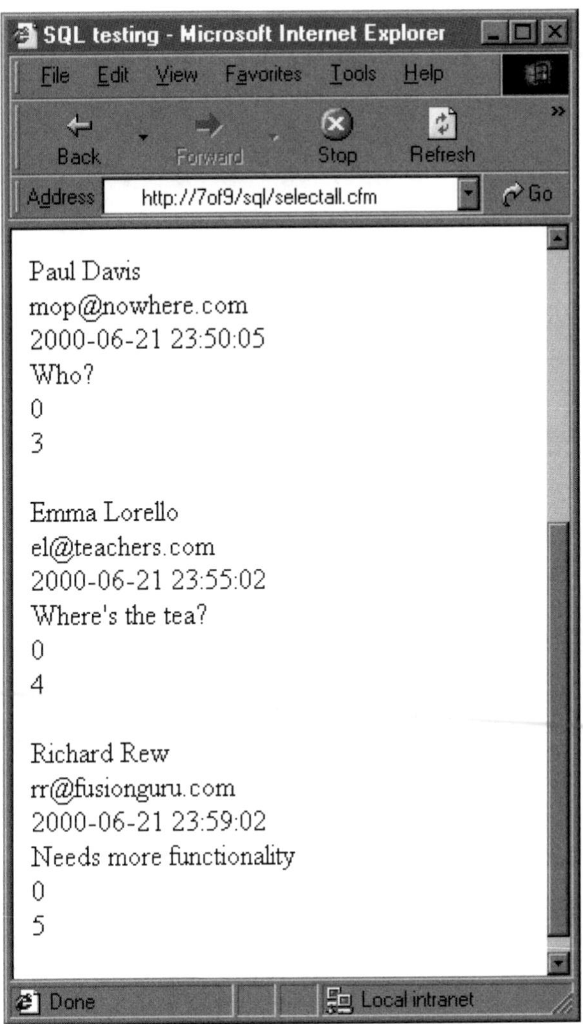

***Figure 5.7** – Sample output from SELECT * statement.*

If you point your browser at the file now it will stop with an error, because the <CFOUTPUT> now refers to several fields that are not returned by the query, so change the code inside the <CFQUERY> tag to:

```
<CFOUTPUT query="SelectALL">
      #ID# #Name#<BR>
</CFOUTPUT>
```

Save the *.cfm* file and reload or refresh the file in the web browser, which should produce a page as shown in figure 5.8.

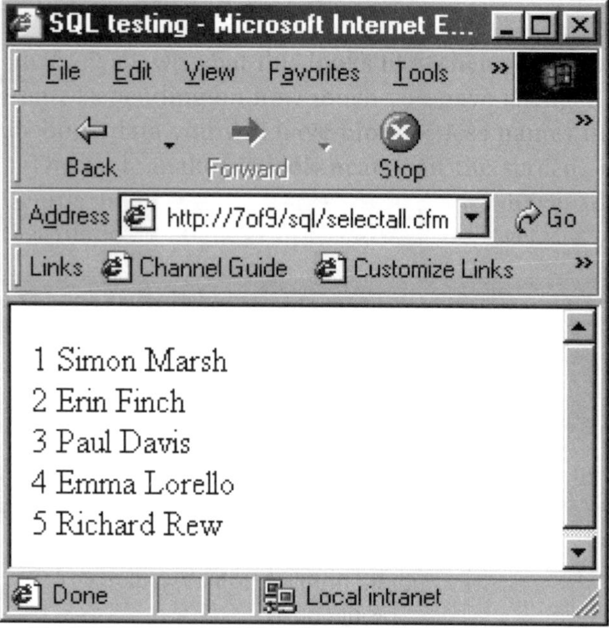

***Figure 5.8** – Select on specific field names.*

Now that you have seen how to select specific fields try selecting some of your own by changing the SQL. Remember that you need to reflect different fields selected in your <CFOUTPUT> if you are to avoid errors. For example, if we were to select the DateAndTime field instead of the name field in the SQL, and forgot to make the change in the <CFOUTPUT> as well it would produce an error as seen in figure 5.9. This is because although the table contains a field called Name, the actual data returned from the query on the database does not, so the <CFOUTPUT> code does not know what the parameter Name refers to.

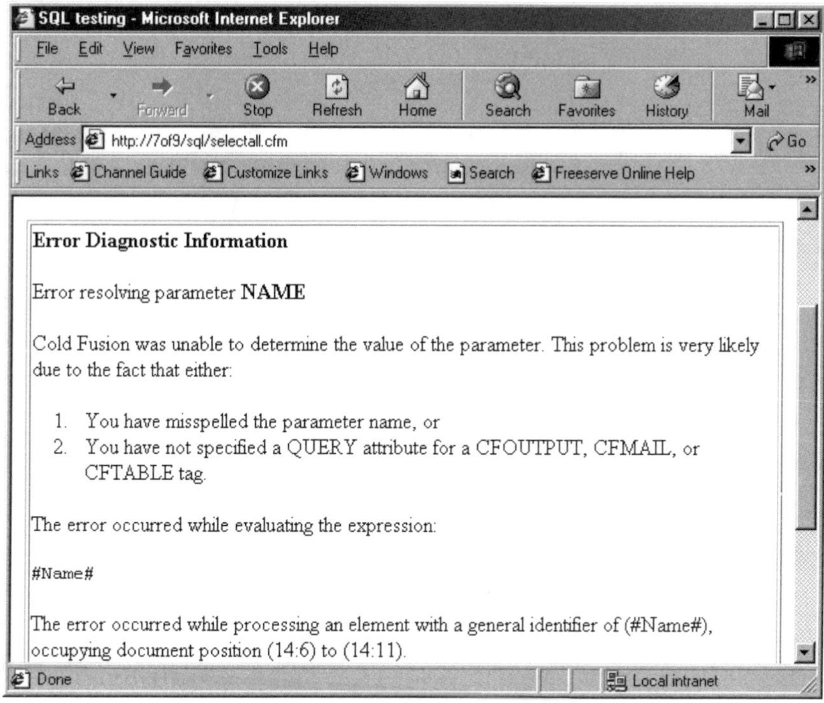

***Figure 5.9** – A ColdFusion error.*

You need to get used to seeing these errors and how to read them, as you will come across several as you are developing applications. Allaire have done a thorough job in developing ColdFusion and generally the errors provide useful feedback. On this occasion the error is useful and can be used to debug our mistake.

After your experimenting, return your code to that which produced the output in figure 5.8:

```
<CFQUERY name="SelectALL" datasource="MyLog">
SELECT      ID,Name
FROM        VisitorBook
</CFQUERY>
<CFOUTPUT query="SelectALL">
#ID# #Name#<BR>
</CFOUTPUT>
```

Append the **SELECT** statement so that it contains a **WHERE** clause as follows:

```
SELECT     ID,Name
FROM       VisitorBook
WHERE      ID = 2
```

Save the *.cfm* file and refresh the page in the browser. The output page should now show the name you have specified as your second visitor. In my case:

```
2 Erin Finch
```

This **WHERE** clause has limited the data so that only records with the ID of 2 are returned. Try changing your code to pull back other records instead of ID 2. There are many other ways to limit the data brought back, so try the following **WHERE** clauses and try and understand the results.

- **WHERE** ID > 2
- **WHERE** NOT ID = 2
- **WHERE** Name **LIKE** 'S%'

Finally in your **SELECT** statement remove the **WHERE** clause completely and replace it with an **ORDER BY** clause so that the complete SQL statement now reads:

```
SELECT     ID,Name
FROM       VisitorBook
ORDER BY   ID ASC
```

Save the file and reload the web page to see the result. Nothing should have changed from figure 5.8, so change the **ORDER BY** line to read:

```
ORDER BY   ID DESC
```

and save and reload the page, this should produce the form shown in figure 5.10.

ORDER BY is not limited to numerical fields, you can order by any field that can be enumerated into an order. So you could use the following lines without a problem:

- **ORDER BY** Name
- **ORDER BY** DateAndTime **DESC**

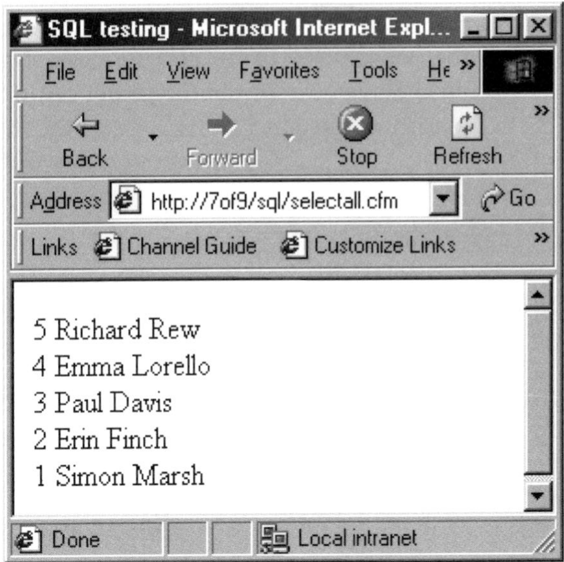

Figure 5.10 – A reverse ordered selection.

The latter is interesting in that you can order by a field that you do not return in the query, the database engine sorts using the field and then returns the requested fields sorted to the query. If you omit the word **DESC** it is assumed that the **ORDER BY** will be **ASC.**

DELETE

Let's assume that someone has made a comment in our visitors' book that we do not like and want to remove the entry via SQL. To remove a record from a table we use the SQL command **DELETE**, which takes the following form:

```
DELETE
FROM      TableName
[WHERE    condition]
```

Unlike the **SELECT** command, this command can be very dangerous as it actually changes the contents of the database. Used without the **WHERE** clause this will remove all of the data from a table, so use the command with caution. Let us remove the third record from the data that we showed in figure 5.10. This person had the name Paul Davis, so we could remove him by executing the following SQL:

```
<CFQUERY name="DeletePaul" datasource="MyLog">
DELETE
FROM        VisitorBook
WHERE       Name = 'Paul Davis'
</CFQUERY>
```

The record could also be deleted with the following:

```
<CFQUERY name="DeletePaul2" datasource="MyLog">
DELETE
FROM        VisitorBook
WHERE       ID = 3
</CFQUERY>
```

In fact any **WHERE** clause that picked out that particular record would delete it. Note that in the last example it would not necessarily delete the third record, it would delete the record whose ID field was equal to the number 3. This is where the primary key in Access being an **AutoNumber** type is useful, as it provides a unique reference to a specific record. Insert the above code into the basic CFM file and save it as *deleteid3.cfm* in the SQL directory of the web server. Now call the file using the web browser by looking at the location:

```
http://WebServerName/sql/deleteid3.cfm
```

Again you will see a blank page. Now reload the page you used in the previous section by calling:

```
http://WebServerName/sql/selectall.cfm
```

With our data we now get the results shown in figure 5.11. Notice that the specified record has been deleted. If we now run the *deleteid3.cfm* file again, and then return to the *selectall.cfm* page, the query does not delete another record, but just returns nothing as there is no record with a primary key of 3 to delete.

***Figure 5.11** – List after deleting ID = 3 record.*

UPDATE

Let's return to our record ID = 1. If you remember we did not add all of the data when we created it. To add or change data in a field in a record that already exists, we use the SQL command UPDATE. The UPDATE command has the following form:

```
UPDATE    TableName
SET       FieldName = Value,
          FieldName2 = Value2, etc
[WHERE    condition];
```

Again this is a potentially dangerous command as it changes data inside the table. In our example, if we were to execute the following command without the **WHERE** clause it could erase all of the data in the *Location* field of all of the records:

```
<CFQUERY name="DeletePaul2" datasource="MyLog">
UPDATE     VisitorBook
SET        Location = 'Skegness'
WHERE      ID = 1;
</CFQUERY>
```

To test the above code place it before the following output code in a base document and save it as *update.cfm*:

```
<CFQUERY name="SelectALL" datasource="MyLog">
Select ID,Name,Location
from VisitorBook
</CFQUERY>
<CFOUTPUT query="SelectALL">
#ID# #Name# #Location#<BR>
</CFOUTPUT>
```

View the *update.cfm* code with your web browser and it will appear as shown in figure 5.12. You will notice that the first record now has a *Location* field in addition to a *Name*, the other records have empty *Location* fields. Finally, if you remove the **WHERE** clause from the **UPDATE** command and save and reload the web page you will see the results as shown in figure 5.13.

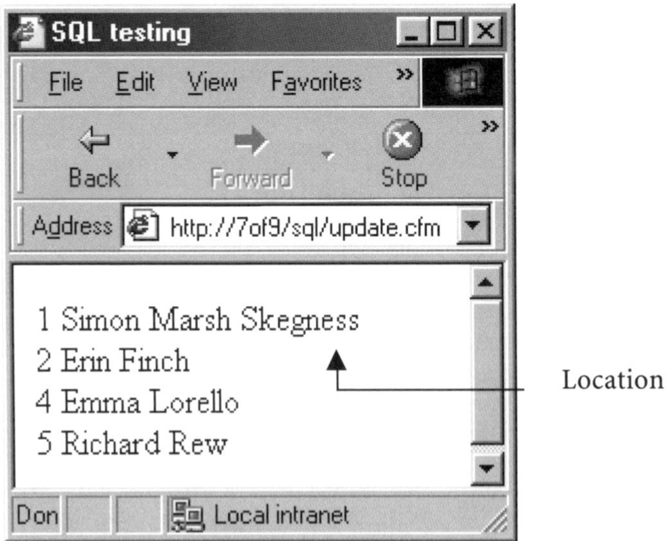

***Figure 5.12** – A selective UPDATE for the first record.*

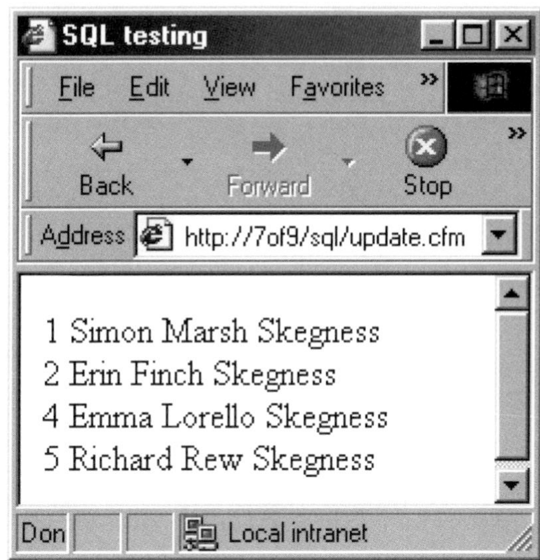

Figure 5.13 *– A global UPDATE for Location.*

This chapter has provided a basic introduction to SQL. The language itself is much more powerful than the simple way that we have used it throughout this chapter. However, most of the database manipulation that you do with ColdFusion will only use the few statements we have covered. If it is your ambition to become a database administration expert then by all means investigate SQL further through one of the many books on the subject.

Chapter

6

Key ColdFusion Tags

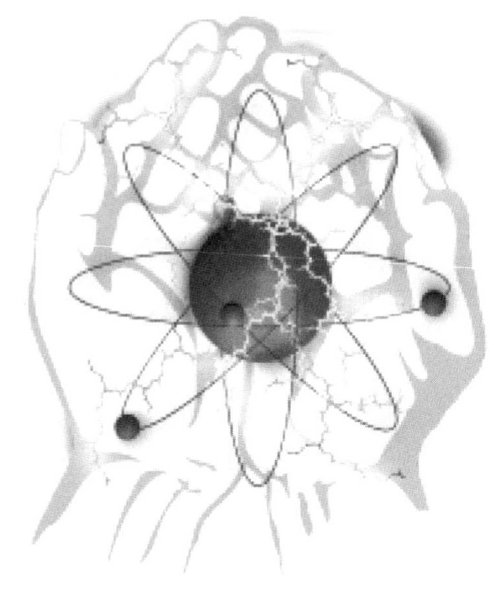

Introduction

The majority of ColdFusion programming is done via tags. A tag in ColdFusion consists of text with a <...> pair as follows:

```
< Tagname [parameters = parametersvalue]>
      [more tag contents]
[</Tagname>]
```

It is similar to a standard HTML tag as described in chapter 4; however, instead of being evaluated by the browser on the client side it is processed by the ColdFusion server. A tag will have a start point, the <*Tagname* > which may contain parameters, it may also have contents, and then it usually has an end tag, which is the tag name proceeded by a / slash.

A full listing of the tags available to you as a ColdFusion programmer, is published in the Allaire *CFML Language Reference Manual.* We have already used several ColdFusion tags, the most notable being <CFQUERY> and <CFOUTPUT>. We will describe these in this chapter applying them into our web site. Tags that fulfil other common functions are grouped together in chapters 7 – 10.

Running SQL with<CFQUERY>

This tag is used to send an SQL query to a database. It takes the following form:

```
<CFQUERY name="queryname"
datasource="nameofdatasource"
maxrows=numberofrowstoreturn
.....>
SQL statement
</CFQUERY>
```

- The **Name** is the token used to refer to the query later on in the *.cfm* template.
- The **Datasource** is the name of the ODBC database that the SQL statement is to be run on.
- **Maxrows** is the maximum number of rows that the query should return. If **maxrows** is omitted the query returns all possible results. For example to get all records in our log table back the tag would be used in the following way:

```
<CFQUERY name="GetRecords" datasource="MyLog">
      SELECT    *
      FROM      Log
</CFQUERY>
```

This would send the SQL code *Select * from Log* to the database engine, which would perform the search and get the data ready for outputting. In this example, all data obtained by the search is prepared as no **maxrows** statement is included. The datasource referenced is the *MyLog* database that we set up in chapter 2.

Although the data is ready for output, no data is returned to the user without a **<CFOUTPUT>** tag that references the query name, which in our example is called *GetRecords*, and the corresponding field names included in the tag. If we add the above code to a base document, and add the **<CFOUTPUT>** tag to output all of the data gained from the search the code is as follows:

```
<HTML>
<TITLE>CFQUERY and CFOUTPUT testfile</TITLE>
<BODY>
<CFQUERY name="GetRecords" datasource="MyLog">
      SELECT    *
      FROM      Log
</CFQUERY>
<CFOUTPUT query="GetRecords">
      |#AccessDateandTime#|#PageName#|#HostName#|< BR>
</CFOUTPUT>
</BODY>
<HTML>
```

Notice how on the <**CFOUTPUT**> statement we have only referenced three of the five fields in that table. However the SQL statement said to get all of the fields, but we can control the amount of data that the system returns through <**CFOUTPUT**>. Make a new directory in the *wwwroot* of your test server called *cftags*, and save the above file as *query1.cfm.*

Once you have done this, view the page using a web browser. It will look similar to figure 6.1 depending on how many hits you have recorded in your database so far.

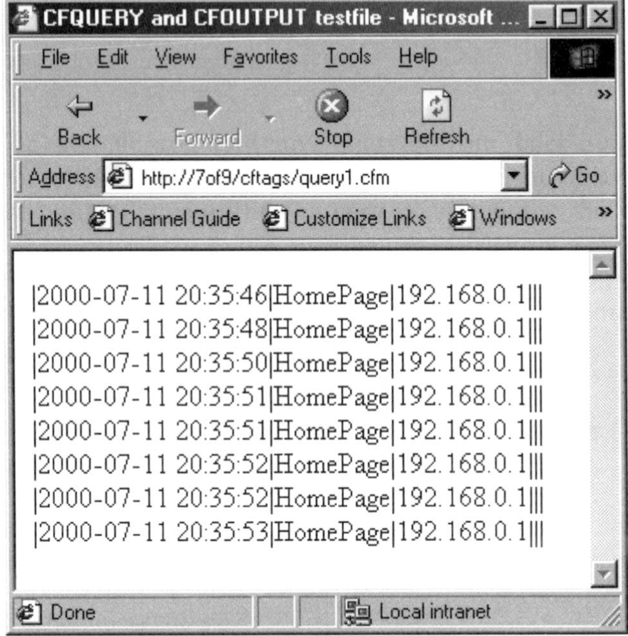

Figure 6.1 *– Sample CFQUERY output.*

Processing with <CFOUTPUT>

The <CFOUTPUT> tag is used to output the results of a database operation or other ColdFusion operation. It takes the following form:

```
<CFOUTPUT query="queryname"
        startrow="TheFirstRowToProcess"
        maxrows=NumberOFRowsToDisplay
        .....>
HTML and ColdFusion code
</CFQUERY>
```

- **query** is the name of the <CFQUERY> that the output is to work on, if needed.
- **maxrows** works the same way as in <CFQUERY> in that it limits the amount of rows that are displayed by the <CFOUTPUT>.
- **startrow** is the first row that the code is to work on, so that you will not always have to start at the very first record, you can move through your data with more control.

The <CFQUERY> works like a loop, executing everything inside the start and end tag for every row of data returned from the query. As can be seen by the previous section, <CFQUERY> and <CFOUTPUT> are often used together; however, all of the parameters in <CFOUTPUT> are optional. For example, the following code

```
<CFOUTPUT>It is #Now()#</CFOUTPUT>
```

refers to no query, but it signifies to ColdFusion that certain data inside the tags need to be evaluated, that is the **Now()** function, which it evaluates and returns the time and the date. If we were to just include the statement :

```
It is #Now()#
```

even inside a *.cfm* file, the ColdFusion server would not evaluate the function and just print:

```
It is #Now()#
```

in the output. The only way you can evaluate ColdFusion variables and functions is inside the <CFOUTPUT> tag or inside another ColdFusion tag.

Load your *query1.cfm* file from the previous section into your editor, and add a *maxrows=2* inside the <CFQUERY> tag just after the *name="GetRecords"*. Save the file and reload into your browser. It should now appear as shown in figure 6.2.

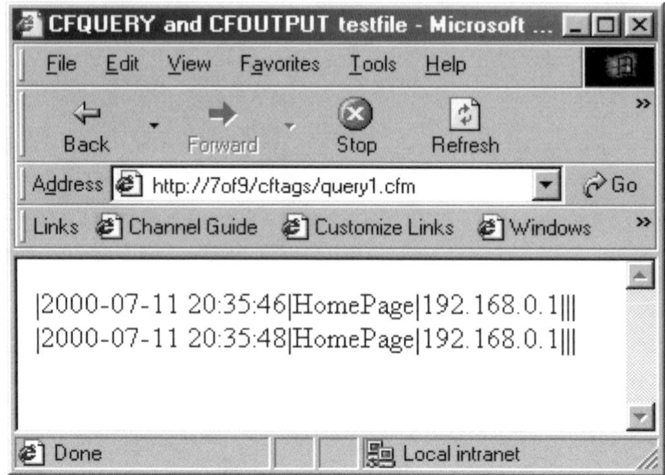

***Figure 6.2** – Output restricted with maxrows.*

Move the **maxrows** statement to the <CFOUTPUT> tag, this time inserting it after the *query="GetRecords"* attribute. Save and reload the page, which will be the same as shown in figure 6.2. **Maxrows** is most useful in the <CFQUERY> tag when you just need to access the query's results once. However, if you were outputting different parts of the query in one template, then **maxrows** is better placed in the <CFOUTPUT> tag.

To illustrate this, consider an Internet Search engine, searching on a popular word, such as *Supermodel.* You may get tens of thousands of results back from that search, you can normally restrict the results to be spread over many pages, that each contain 25 results. A link on the page takes you to the next set of results. Such a results set could easily be created using the **maxrows** and **startrow** properties of the <CFOUTPUT> tag in ColdFusion. To demonstrate, edit your *query1.cfm* file to:

```
<HTML>
<TITLE>startrow and maxrow </TITLE>
<BODY>
```

```
<CFQUERY name="GetRecords" datasource="MyLog">
    SELECT    *
    FROM      Log
</CFQUERY>
<P>Here are the first 2 results:<BR>
<CFOUTPUT query="GetRecords" maxrows=2 >
    |#AccessDateandTime#|#PageName#|
    #HostIPNum#|#HostName#|#Browser#|<BR>
</CFOUTPUT>
<P>Here are the next 2 results:<BR>
<CFOUTPUT query="GetRecords" startrow=3 maxrows=2 >
    |#AccessDateandTime#|#PageName#|
    #HostIPNum#|#HostName#|#Browser#|<BR>
</CFOUTPUT>
<P>And the next 2:<BR>
<CFOUTPUT query="GetRecords" startrow=5 maxrows=2 >
    |#AccessDateandTime#|#PageName#|
    #HostIPNum#|#HostName#|#Browser#|<BR>
</CFOUTPUT>
    <CFOUTPUT>Total visits: #GetRecords.RecordCount# </CFOUTPUT>
</BODY>
<HTML>
```

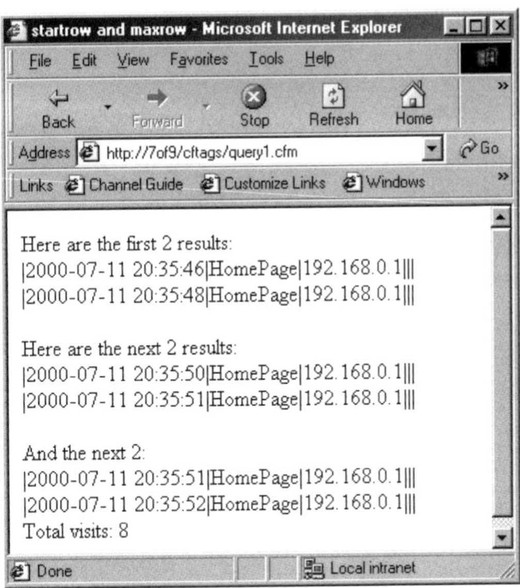

*Figure 6.3 – Output controlled using **startrow** and **maxrow**.*

The above code will generate the page shown in figure 6.3. All of the <CFOUTPUT> tags use different subsets of the data returned by the single <CFQUERY>. The last <CFOUTPUT> refers to no query set, but instead a special variable called **RecordCount**, that returns the number of records that the query returned.

Figure 6.3 shows a simplified use of the **startrow** and **maxrows** attributes of <CFOUTPUT> when all of the data is displayed on the same page. If this was the result of a search engine output the results would be spread over many pages and so different code would be required to control the **startrow** attribute.

Chapter 7

Forms and Formatting

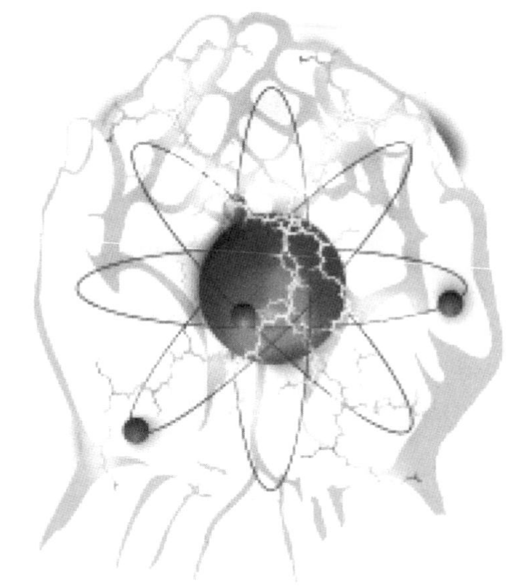

Introduction

To make a web site interactive we need to obtain information from the user. We have already obtained information about their visit without their knowledge. To get information from them in a less covert way, we use a form. If you are a web user you probably use forms everyday without noticing, each time you use a search engine, such as Google, shown in figure 7.1.

The form is recognized by having:

- Somewhere for the user to enter data, by means of the **Enter search terms** box in figure 7.1, or the **All Languages** drop down selector next to it.
- A button, or buttons, which tell the web browser that you've finished entering the data and wish to do something with it.

ColdFusion's Forms <CFFORM>

HTML has a FORM tag built in which was outlined in chapter 4, but in ColdFusion there is a special implementation of it with added features called <CFFORM>. Some of the <CFFORM> functionality is provided through JavaScript, so if your browser does not support this you have to use the HTML version of FORM. The <CFFORM> will usually be held in one template file, and the code needed to process its data is in another file that the form will send its information to once it has been submitted.

<CFFORM> takes the following format:

```
<CFFORM name="formName"
action="templateName"
...>
	HTML code, CFFORM control tags
</CFFORM>
```

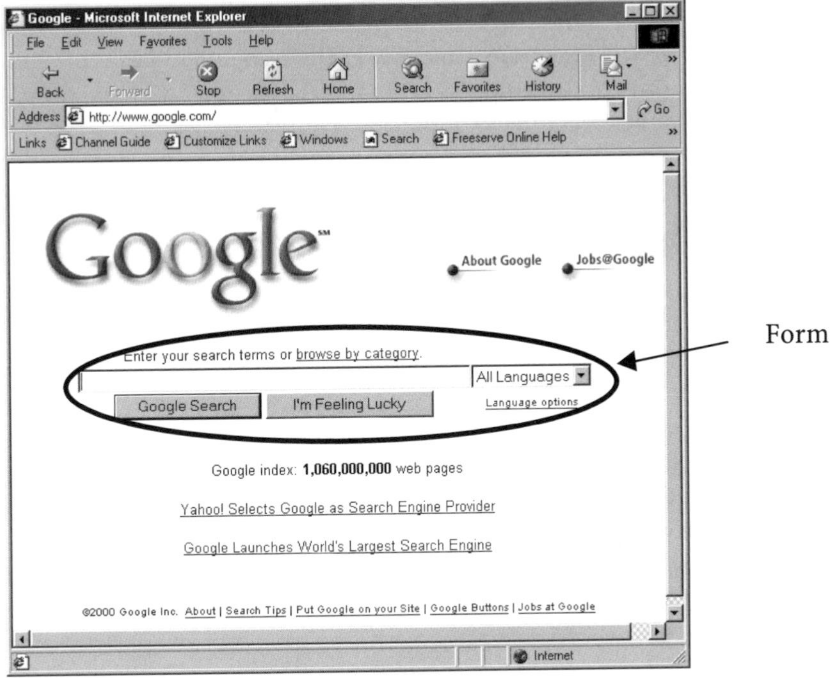

Figure 7.1 – A form in the middle of the Google search engine.

- **name** is the name of the form to refer to in later template files.
- **action** is the *.cfm* file that will be executed once the form has been submitted.

Components of a form such as the text box or submit button are known as control tags. Some common ColdFusion variants are:

- <CFINPUT>, which creates an input section of the form, which could be a text box, radio button or checkbox.
- <CFTEXTINPUT>, which creates a larger area when the user can enter text.
- <CFSELECT>, which creates a drop down box such as the **All Languages** box in figure 6.1.

You can also use the standard HTML form tags inside the <CFFORM>, for example to create a submit button.

To demonstrate the use of <CFFORM> we will develop our visitor book function of the web site to get some more information from the user. To begin with, we need to investigate the <CFINPUT> control tag.

Input control <CFINPUT>

This is used to create an input section inside a <CFFORM>. It takes the following format:

```
<CFINPUT TYPE="typeOfControl"
NAME="nameOfControl"
VALUE="ValueWhenCreated"
REQUIRED="YES/NO"
RANGE="minimum, maximum"
VALIDATE="typeOfData"
MESSAGE="ValidationFailMessage"
SIZE="size"
MAXLENGTH="Length"
CHECKED="Yes/No"
>
```

Name is the only required attribute of the <CFINPUT> tag, but you will find that you have to use **type** as well. Almost all of the other attributes are used to validate the data that the user has entered.

Type signifies what sort of input you are creating. Type has to be one of the following:

- **Text.** A small text entry box.
- **Radio.** A radio button.
- **Checkbox.** A checkbox that can be either checked – on – or not checked – off.
- **Password.** A small text entry box in which the contents appear as stars when typed.

Type the following into a *.cfm* file and save it as *form1.cfm* in your *cftags* directory of your web server:

```
<HTML>
<HEAD>
	<TITLE>CFFORM Input demos</TITLE>
```

```
</HEAD>
<BODY>
	<CFFORM name="form1" action="form2.cfm">
		<CFINPUT type="Text" Name="textboxone">
		<CFINPUT type="Radio" Name="radioone" value="Radio1">
		<CFINPUT type="Checkbox" Name="checkboxone">
		<CFINPUT type="Password" Name="passwordone">
	</CFFORM>
</BODY>
</HTML>
```

Figure 7.2 shows the output of this code when viewed with a browser.

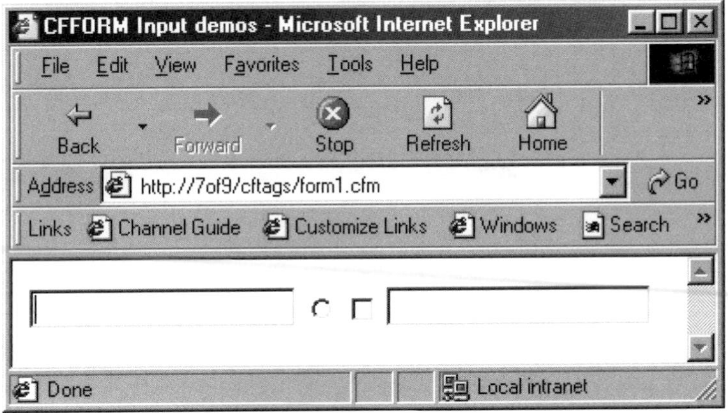

Figure 7.2 – *Several controls in a <CFFORM>.*

If you type the word *Hello* into both boxes you will notice how the password box substitutes the letters typed by asterisks. Notice that although the ColdFusion code is set out neatly, the actual processing of the form simply occurs from left to right across the page, which is not very readable, and also, because there are no captions, the form is meaningless as the user does not know what he is being asked to type.

To fix this problem, alter the <CFFORM> tags contents so that it reads as follows:

```
	<CFFORM name="form1" action="form2.cfm">
Enter some text:
<CFINPUT type="Text" Name="textboxone"><BR>
```

```
        A Radio Button:
        <CFINPUT type="Radio"
            Name="radioone" value="Radio1"><BR>
        A Checkbox:
        <CFINPUT type="Checkbox"
            Name="checkboxone"><BR>
        Enter a Password:
        <CFINPUT type="Password"
            Name="passwordone"><BR>
    </cfform>
```

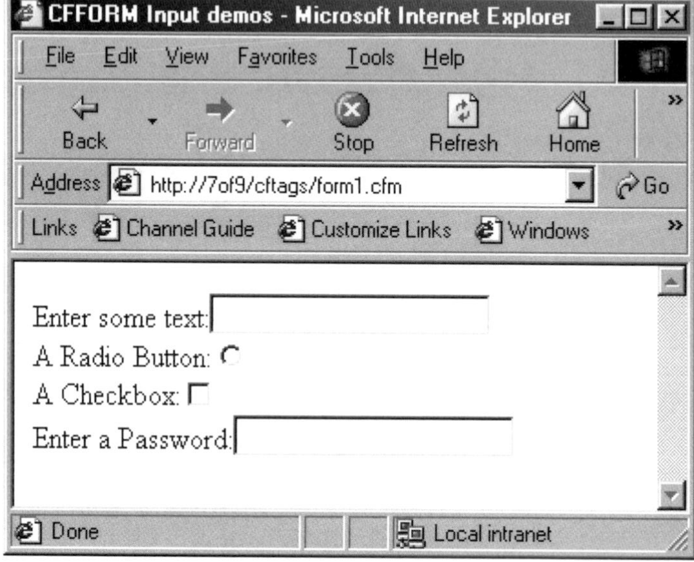

***Figure 7.3** – <CFFORM> – basic formatting and legends.*

Figure 7.3 shows what this looks like, which is rather neater but it would be better if these controls all lined up. The easiest way to accomplish this is to put a table inside the <CFFORM>. Chapter 4 described how the table tag works, but to quickly implement the table change your *form1.cfm* file to read as follows:

```
<HTML>
<HEAD>
    <TITLE>CFFORM Input demos</TITLE>
</HEAD>
```

```
<BODY>
    <CFFORM name="form1" action="form2.cfm">
    <TABLE>
        <TR>
        <TD>Enter some text:</TD>
        <TD><CFINPUT type="Text" Name="textboxone"></TD></TR>
        <TR>
        <TD>A Radio Button:</TD>
        <TD><CFINPUT type="Radio" Name="radioone"
                    value="Radio1"></TD></TR>
        <TR>
        <TD>A Checkbox:</TD>
        <TD><CFINPUT type="Checkbox"
                    Name="checkboxone"></TD></TR>
        <TR>
        <TD>Enter a Password:</TD>
        <TD><CFINPUT type="Password"
                    Name="passwordone"></TD></TR>
    </TABLE>
    </CFFORM>
</BODY>
</HTML>
```

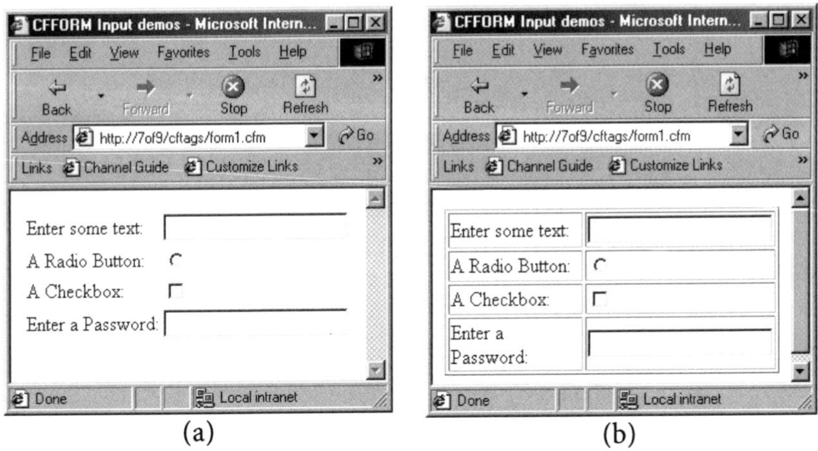

***Figure 7.4** – How a table controls layout within a <CFFORM>.*

Figure 7.4a shows what this code looks like when viewed. The borders of the table are highlighted in figure 7.4b to show just how the table is controlling the text inside it. To get the effect of figure 7.4b yourself just add *Border=1* inside the <TABLE …> tag.

Validating Input with <CFFORM>

Next we will see one of the ways that <CFFORM> differs from FORM in HTML, that of input validation. To maintain meaningful data we have to control how the user enters it.

For example, if we were asking for an address, we would not want the user to put a telephone number in the Postal/Zip code box, or their street address in the telephone field. You could validate the data on the template file that receives the data, and if it was incorrect return the user to the original page. However, this can require complex programming so it is much better to force the user into typing the correct response before continuing.

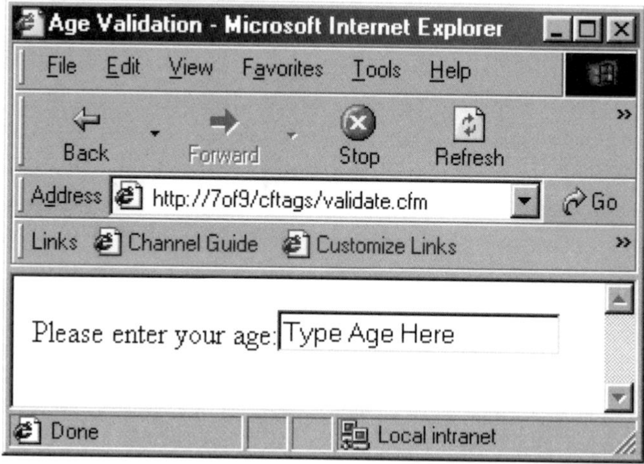

Figure 7.5 – Validating an age.

Examine figure 7.5 which is created using the following code saved as *validate.cfm*:

```
<HTML>
<HEAD>
```

```
    <TITLE>Age Validation</TITLE>
</HEAD>
<BODY>
    <CFFORM name="validate1" action="validate2.cfm">
        Please enter your age:
        <CFINPUT type="Text" Name="age"
        Value="Type Age Here"><BR>
    </cfform>
</BODY>
</HTML>
```

The code produces a field that is waiting for a number that represents the user's age in years, but that may not be obvious to the user. Remember that the field is just a text field, so any of the following could be typed in:

- Nothing
- 24
- I'm 24
- Harold
- Twenty Four
- -42
- Not telling you
- Type Age Here

The list could continue for many more options. Only one, the number 24 would be meaningful in this context, and yet a standard form would let all of them through, causing the next template file that processes them to crash with an error. To trap this error, we need to set an acceptable range for our age, say 0–110 years, and a data type, which is an integer (whole number). If we use an integer, we will not be concerned with fractions of years. To validate this range, we need to add the following attributes to inside the <CFINPUT> tag:

```
validate="integer"
range="0,110"
```

This checks that this field is an integer within the range of 0 and 110. Reload the form after making these changes and try and type *I'm 24* into the field. You will get the response shown in figure 7.6. Try typing in some of the other incorrect data and watch how it traps the error in a similar range. When you do type a correct age in, you will get a further different error, this time from the ColdFusion server. Read the error and see if you can understand what it is telling you and why it occurs.

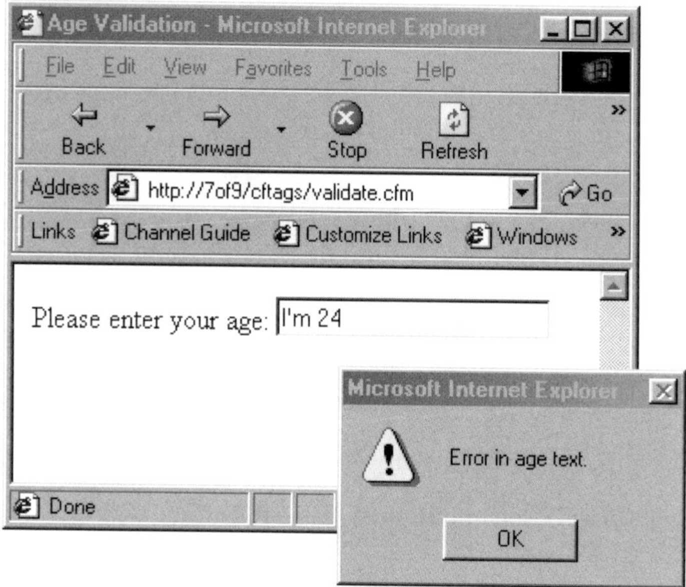

Figure 7.6 – A successfully trapped out of range age.

Look again at the error in figure 7.6. Notice that it says "Error in age text", which is not very friendly as the user has made the obvious mistake of typing text and a number. It is good practice to give a more meaningful feedback to correct the error. We can add a further bit of functionality into our <CFINPUT> tag by adding the following inside the tag:

```
message = "The age must be a whole number, in years between 0 and 110"
```

The output of this is shown in figure 7.7, which will appear if you try and type something wrong into the box again after saving the modified code.

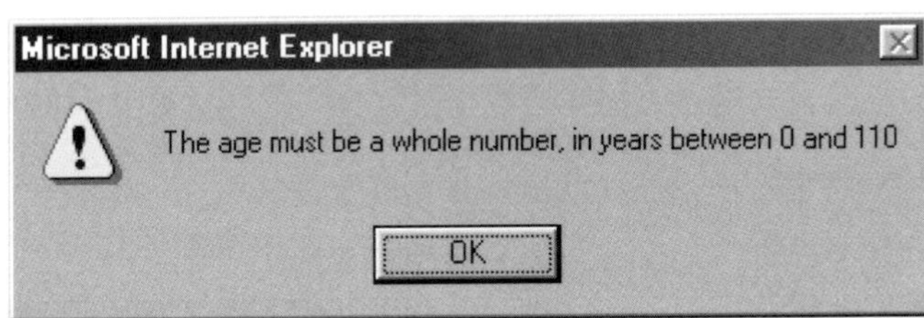

Figure 7.7 – A more meaningful input validation error.

To recap: <CFFORM> has more functionality than FORM as it provides a method of validating entry at the input stage. The complete <INPUT> tag for our age field will be as follows:

```
<CFINPUT type="Text" Name="age"
        Value="Type Age Here"
        validate="integer"
        range="0,110"
        message = "The age must be a
        whole number, in years
        between 0 and 110" >
```

This stops the user from entering anything other than a whole number between 0 and 110 and if they do gives them an error message that explains what is expected from them. The validate attribute is not just limited to integers and can check for other types of data such as:

- **Date** – US date format mm/dd/yyyy.
- **Eurodate** – European date format dd/mm/yyyy.
- **Time** – in the format hh:mm:ss.
- **Float** – a floating point number.
- **Telephone** – Regional to US format phone numbers.
- **Zipcode** – Regional to US format postal codes.
- **Creditcard** - Strips blanks and hyphens and checks number via the mod10 credit card number algorithm.
- **Social_security_number** – Regional to US format social security numbers ###-##-####.

There are other methods of validating input via the form using JavaScript. Consult the Allaire ColdFusion manuals for how to do this.

Font control and <CFTEXTINPUT>

<CFTEXTINPUT> is very similar to the <CFINPUT type= “text”> tag. In addition to the validation functions described earlier this tag also allows full control over the font, size, file, colour and alignment of the input text.

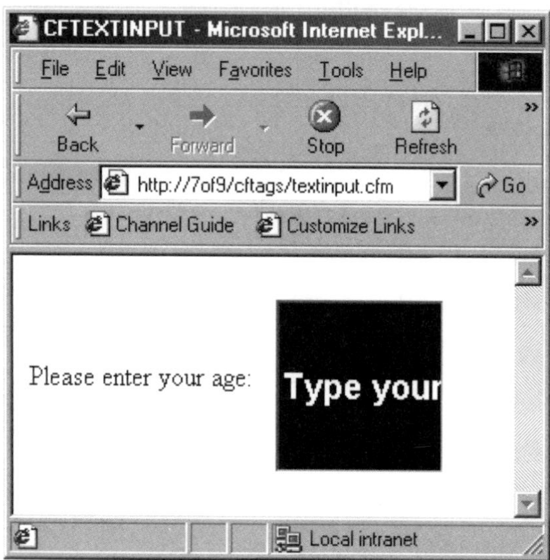

Figure 7.8 – <CFTEXTINPUT> on our age validation code.

<CFTEXTINPUT> takes the following format:

```
<CFTEXTINPUT NAME=" nameOfControl "
  VALUE=" ValueWhenCreated "
  REQUIRED=" YES/NO "
  RANGE="minimum, maximum"
  VALIDATE=" typeOfData "
  MESSAGE=" ValidationFailMessage "
  SIZE="sizeofbox"
  FONT="NameOfFont"
  FONTSIZE="SizeOfFont"
```

```
ITALIC="YES/NO"
BOLD="YES/NO"
HEIGHT="HeightofControl(pixels)"
WIDTH="WidthofControl(pixels)"
VSPACE="integer(pixels)"
HSPACE="integer(pixels)"
ALIGN="alignment"
BGCOLOR="colour"
TEXTCOLOR="colour"
MAXLENGTH="length"
NOTSUPPORTED="text"
>
```

Most of these attributes have been described earlier, and the font control and colour attributes should be familiar to the HTML user. Figure 7.8 shows how the following code when saved as *textinput.cfm* is rendered in a web browser:

```
<HTML>
<HEAD>
    <TITLE>CFTEXTINPUT</TITLE>
</HEAD>
<BODY>
    <CFFORM name="age1" action="age2.cfm">
        Please enter your age:
        <CFTEXTINPUT NAME="age"
          VALUE="Type your age here"
          RANGE="0, 110"
          VALIDATE="integer"
          SIZE="10"
          FONT="Comic Sans MS"
          FONTSIZE="20"
          ITALIC="NO"
          BOLD="YES"
          HEIGHT="100"
          WIDTH="100"
          VSPACE="10"
          HSPACE="10"
          ALIGN="center"
          BGCOLOR="black"
          TEXTCOLOR="white"
          MAXLENGTH="3"
          >
    </CFFORM>
```

```
</BODY>
</HTML>
```

Although you may think that this tag is complex, it really saves you lots of coding at a deeper level. Using your browser, view the source code of the file that generates figure 7.8. You will see from the resulting page that ColdFusion has written pages and pages of JavaScript for you to do what looked like simple text formatting and validation!

List controls with <CFSELECT>

<CFSELECT> creates a control in a form that contains a list of elements for the user to select. The user can select one or many from the list depending on the options set in the tag. The tag takes on the following format:

```
<CFSELECT NAME="NameOfControl"
        REQUIRED="Yes/No"
        MESSAGE="text"
        ONERROR="text"
        SIZE="SizeOfControl"
        MULTIPLE="Yes/No"
        QUERY="queryname"
        SELECTED="ColumnValue"
        VALUE="ColumnName"
        DISPLAY="text">
    </CFSELECT>
```

- **Required** is the same as in other controls, and if set to *yes*, ensures that the user selects at least one element from the list. If they do not, the browser displays the text included in the **Message** attribute.
- **Size** is the number of lines on the screen that the control displays at once. If there are more elements than lines, a scroll control appears.
- If **Multiple** is set to yes, the user can select more than one element. If no, only one element is allowed.

- **Query** is the name of the query that the control gets its list from. If this is omitted then the control gets its list from the <OPTION> tag discussed in the next section.
- **Value** is used to select the column name in the query that the control returns. This is not necessarily the column that is displayed.
- **Selected** allows you to preselect a value from the list so that the user can leave it as it is or make their own selection.
- **Display** is the column name in the query that is actually displayed to the user that they can select from.

This sounds very complex until you see it in action. We will use the data we set up in the visitor book section to populate the list. Type the following code into an editor and save as *cfselect.cfm*

```
<HTML>
<HEAD>
    <TITLE>CFSELECT</TITLE>
</HEAD>
<BODY>
    <CFQUERY datasource="MyLog" name="GetVisitors">
        select *
        from Visitorbook
    </CFQUERY>
    <TABLE>
    <CFFORM name="select" action="cfselect2.cfm">
        <TR><TD valign="top">Please Select Visitor:</TD>
        <TD><CFSELECT NAME="Visitor"
          REQUIRED="Yes"
          MESSAGE="Select one name"
          SIZE="7"
          MULTIPLE="No"
          QUERY="GetVisitors"
          VALUE="ID"
          DISPLAY="Name">
        </CFSELECT>
        </td></tr>
        <TR><TD></td><TD>
            <INPUT type="submit" value="GetDetails">
```

```
        </td></tr>
    </cfform>
    </table>
</BODY>
</HTML>
```

Figure 7.9 shows what this looks like when run in a web browser. Depending on how much you have changed our visitor book data you will have more or less names in the box. The table makes it look neater on the screen. The GetDetails button will not work until we have added another file so do not be tempted to click on it yet.

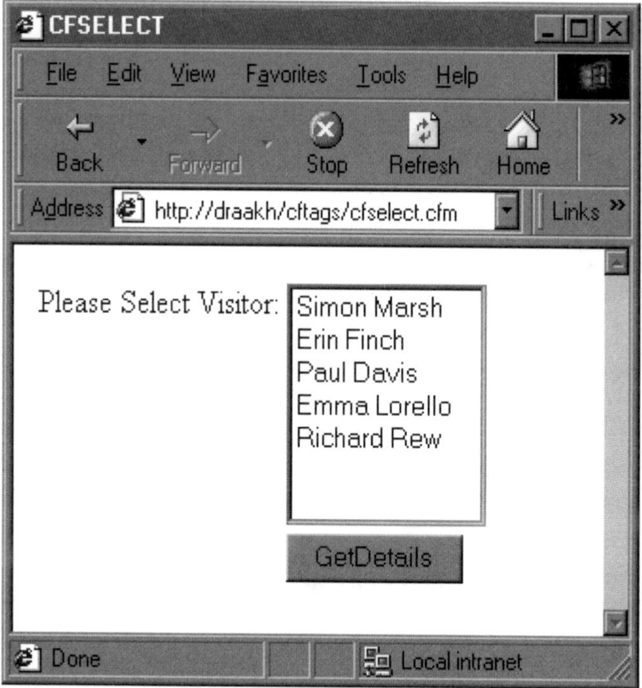

***Figure 7.9** – Select box with elements sourced from a query.*

Notice how the **size** attribute has made the box big enough to display seven items at once, but the query has only returned five in our example. Although we are only working with small numbers this will prevent your web pages from becoming unwieldy when you have lots of records to display. To get the submit button working save the following code as *cfselect2.cfm:*

```
<HTML>
<HEAD>
	<TITLE>CFSELECT</TITLE>
</HEAD>
<BODY>
	<CFQUERY datasource="MyLog" name="GetVisitorDetails">
		select *
		from Visitorbook
		where ID=#Form.Visitor#
	</CFQUERY>
	<TABLE>
	<CFOUTPUT query="GetVisitorDetails">
		<TR><TD>ID</td><TD>#ID#</td></tr>
		<TR><TD>Name</td><TD>#Name#</td></tr>
		<TR><TD>Email</td><TD>#Email#</td></tr>
		<TR><TD>Comment</td><TD>#Comment#</td></tr>
		<TR><TD>DateAndTime</td><TD>#DateAndTime#</td></tr>
		<TR><TD>Location</td><TD>#Location#</td></tr>
	</CFOUTPUT>
	</table>
	<A href="cfselect.cfm">View Another</A>
</BODY>
</HTML>
```

Figure 7.10 shows the results when you now press the GetDetails button in figure 7.9. If you look at the code you will notice that although the user selects the name; in this case *Emma Lorello*; the <CFSELECT> sends the ID field; in our case the value *4*, through to the next page. This makes the search that we have to do easier, as we just have to search for the ID number in the <CFQUERY> in the *cfselect.cfm* file. In this way, the <CFSELECT> statement gives you the opportunity to give the user a more friendly interface while still having the opportunity to perform more technical searches with the results.

***Figure 7.10** – Select results.*

Many choices with <OPTION>

There are times, however, when we need a list box but do not wish to populate it with data held in a database. We can hardcode the data into the <CFSELECT> by using the standard HTML tag <OPTION>. This takes the following form:

```
<CFSELECT ...
     select attributes>
          <Option>Listbox element 1</Option>
          <Option>Listbox element 2</Option>
          ...
</CFSELECT>
```

To use this tag you set up a <CFSELECT> as in the previous example but omit any of the attributes that refer to a query. Then you add each element of the list between the <CFSELECT> start and end tags within the <OPTION> tag. For example, the following code will add a location dialogue to our visitor book to select where the user lives.

```
<HTML>
<HEAD>
      <TITLE>CFSELECT with Option</TITLE>
</HEAD>
<BODY>
      <TABLE>
      <CFFORM name="optiontest" action="option.cfm">
            <TR><TD valign="top">Where do you come from?:</TD>
            <TD>
            <CFSELECT NAME="Location"
              REQUIRED="Yes"
              SIZE="5"
              MULTIPLE="No">
                        <OPTION>UK</OPTION>
                        <OPTION>US</OPTION>
                        <OPTION>Canada</OPTION>
                        <OPTION>France</OPTION>
                        <OPTION>Not Listed</OPTION>
            </CFSELECT>
            </td></tr>
      </cfform>
      </table>
</BODY>
</HTML>
```

Figure 7.11 shows the above code when saved as *cfoption.cfm* and ran through a browser. When options are hard coded into the template file like above they become less useful to a dynamic web site.

For instance, your web site may suddenly start getting lots of visitors from Germany, so to add this to the list would require a rewrite of the above code. If, however, you were populating the list from a query, your code could:

- Identify visitors from a country that was not listed.
- Prompt the user for the new country.

- Amend the database of countries.
- Present this new country to any further visitors.

This way your site becomes customized to your users with little input from yourself. This is one of the major benefits of having a database behind your web sites.

***Figure 7.11** – Using <OPTION> to populate <CFSELECT>.*

Chapter 8 Looping and Branching

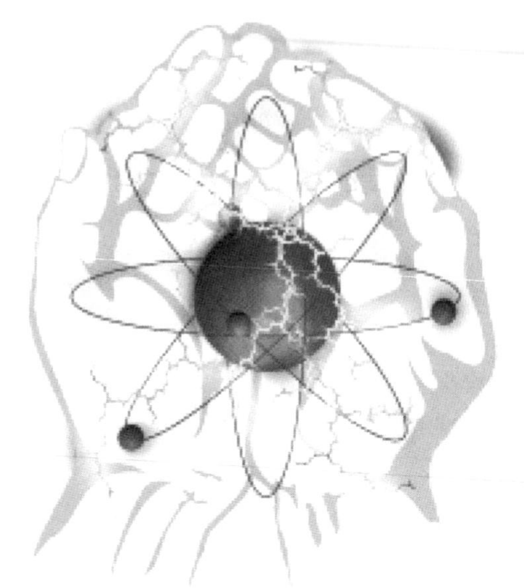

Introduction

There are times when you want to get your browser, or your HTML, to perform repetitive tasks. In this situation it is sometimes easier to tell the ColdFusion server to step through a series of tags repeatedly until a certain condition is met.

The <CFLOOP> command is used to accomplish this. If you are familiar with other programming languages you may find it interesting that all of the common looping constructs are implemented in ColdFusion within the one tag, as opposed to having a different command for differently controlled loops. Therefore, there is not one standard format for a <CFLOOP> tag as different attributes used determine the type of loop that is to be executed. The most commonly used loop types are:

- Index loops.
- Conditional loops.
- Looping over the results of a query.

We will describe the above types of loop in the next sections. Other more specialized loops are explained in Allaire's *CFML Language Reference* manual.

Another powerful method of adding interaction to web sites is by making decisions. Different results are displayed depending on predetermined criteria. This chapter continues by describing some of the tags that control branching in ColdFusion, namely:

- <CFIF>
- <CFELSEIF>
- <CFELSE>
- <CFSWITCH>

<CFLOOP> Index Loops

This loop is used when you wish to loop through a range of numbers and have a definite start and end value. This has the following format:

```
<CFLOOP INDEX="VariableName" FROM="StartValue"
	TO="EndValue"
	STEP="StepValue" >
		....HTML and CFML to loop through...
</CFLOOP>
```

- **Index** is the variable name which stores the current value of the numbers you are stepping through which you can refer to in your code later.
- **From** and **To** are the first and last number that you want to deal with.
- **Step** is the increment you use to work through the numbers. Normally this is 1, which is the default value if **Step** is omitted.

For example if you wanted to give your visitors the opportunity to select the year of their birth on your visitors book, from a range of 1920–1999, you could use the following index loop:

```
<HTML>
<HEAD>
	<TITLE>Index Loop</TITLE>
</HEAD>
<BODY>
What year were you born?
<SELECT Name="YearOfBirth">
	<CFLOOP INDEX="Year" FROM="1920" TO="1999">
		<CFOUTPUT>
			<OPTION>#Year#</OPTION>
		</CFOUTPUT>
	</CFLOOP>
</SELECT>
</BODY>
</HTML>
```

Using a loop of this kind stops you having to put seventy <OPTION> lines in your code, one for each year. Incidentally that's just what the ColdFusion server does. Try saving the above as *indexloops.cfm* and viewing it in your browser, as shown in figure 8.1.

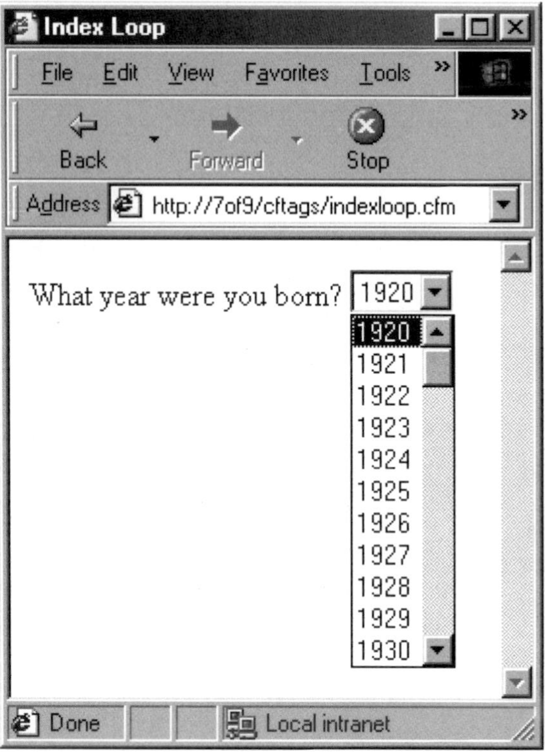

Figure 8.1 *– Dropdown list using an Indexed <CFLOOP>.*

Once you have looked at the pull down list select **View Source** from your browser menu and you will see that the HTML that you have generated does indeed contain 70 <OPTION> lines. At least we did not have to type it!

If you look again at figure 8.1 you will see that the years are listed from the earliest. If we were writing user friendly web pages it might be easier for the user if we were to list it with more recent years first. To do that we need to put the following attributes in the <CFLOOP> tag:

```
<CFLOOP INDEX="Year"
    FROM="1999"
    TO="1920"
    STEP="-1">
```

In this case we are stepping backwards through the years, so the **step** value is *-1*. We also need to remember to change the start and end values. The step value does not even have to be an integer. Try a step of *-0.5* in the above example and see if you can predict the results.

<CFLOOP> Conditional Loops

In the previous example we stepped through a predefined set of values. Sometimes we may need some code to repeat until something happens, or something changes. An example of this is the program that senses key presses on your computer. The program loops waiting for a key to be pressed, as soon as it does, the loop ends and the program goes off and does something else. The conditional loop version of <CFLOOP> is as follows:

```
<CFLOOP CONDITION="test">
```

- ***test*** is the condition that you are checking for.

We could rewrite our previous select statement using a conditional loop as follows:

```
<SELECT Name="YearOfBirth">
    <CFSET Year=1930>
    <CFLOOP CONDITION ="Year LT 2000">
        <CFOUTPUT>
            <OPTION>#Year#</OPTION>
        </CFOUTPUT>
        <CFSET Year = Year+1>
    </CFLOOP>
</SELECT>
```

In this example we use a variable called *year*, which we set at the value 1930 before we begin the loop. You can learn more about variables in chapter 11. Every time the loop is executed:

- It checks to see if the variable *year* is less than 2000.
  - ➢ If it is not the loop ends and processing continues after the </CFLOOP> tag.
  - ➢ If variable *year* is less than 2000 it inserts the OPTION tag with the current year into the **Select** statement and increments the year variable by one.
- It then repeats the code again if needed.

The output is the same as our previous loop example as shown in figure 8.1.

<CFLOOP> Looping over a query

<CFLOOP> can also repeat a series of instructions for every, or some, lines of a query. This is very similar to the <CFOUTPUT> tag when applied to a query, but it allows you to use tags that are not valid inside <CFOUTPUT>. The format of this version of <CFLOOP> is as follows:

```
<CFLOOP query="NameOfQuery"
    startrow="StartingRowNumber"
    endrow="EndingRowNumber">
```

- **query** is the name of the query that we will be running the loop on.
- **startrow** and **endrow** are optional and are used if you wish to further restrict the contents of the query loop by specifying the starting and ending row.

We have previously used the ColdFusion variable **RecordCount** to count the number of rows in the query. We can, however, demonstrate how this is done on our visitor book database by using <CFLOOP> as follows.

```
<HTML>
<HEAD>
    <TITLE>Query CFLOOP</TITLE>
```

```
</HEAD>
<BODY>
    <CFQUERY datasource = "MyLog" name="VBook">
        Select * from VisitorBook
    </CFQUERY>
    <CFSET Visitors=0>
    <CFLOOP query="VBook">
        <CFOUTPUT>#Name#<BR></CFOUTPUT>
        <CFSET Visitors=Visitors+1>
    </CFLOOP>
    <CFOUTPUT>#Visitors# have placed an entry
            in the visitor's book</CFOUTPUT>
</BODY>
</HTML>
```

First of all this code selects all of the records from our visitor book database. We then use a variable called *Visitors* that is set to zero before running through the loop. The loop prints the name of the visitor that it is looking at and then adds one to the visitors variable. It repeats this for every other record of the query. After the loop finishes, we print out the visitors variable to give the number of entries in our book as shown in figure 8.2.

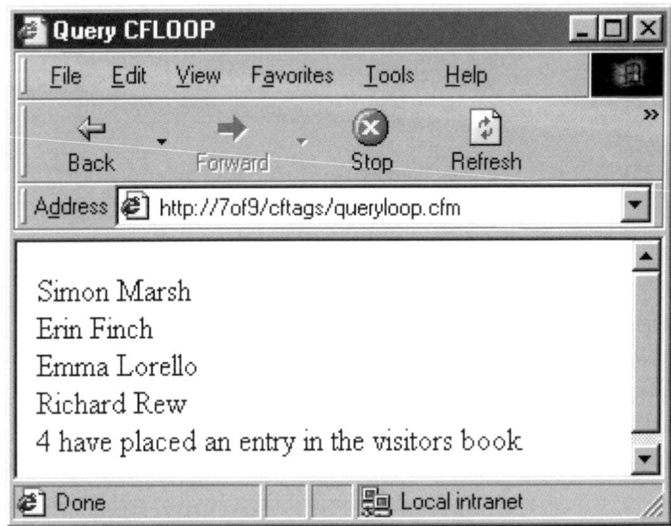

***Figure 8.2** – CFLOOP looping through a query result.*

Branching with <CFIF>

One of the most powerful ways of making a dynamic web site is by making the page change based on decisions on that page or contents of the underlying database. Most programming languages have a method of running different pieces of code based on a decision. ColdFusion is no exception and it has implemented this branching in the tag <CFIF> which takes the following format:

```
<CFIF condition>
	CFML and HTML code executed if condition is true
</CFIF>
```

For example, you may run a query on your database that at some time returns no results. You could just leave it blank, but this would not be very user friendly. So you could use a <CFIF> tag to give the user a friendly message if there were no results. The following code is an example of this, and will work as long as you do not have a visitor in your visitor book called *Christopher Bowers*:

```
<HTML>
<HEAD>
	<TITLE>CFIF one</TITLE>
</HEAD>
<BODY>
<CFQUERY datasource = "MyLog" name="Getdetails">
	Select * from VisitorBook
	where Name = 'Christopher Bowers'
</CFQUERY>
<CFOUTPUT query="GetDetails">#ID# #Name# #Location#</CFOUTPUT>
<CFIF Getdetails.Recordcount LT 1>
Sorry, No records were found
</cfif>
</BODY>
</HTML>
```

If this person did exist in your visitor book then you would see his name, his entry ID and his Location details on the screen. If not, then without the <CFIF> you would see nothing. This is because <CFOUTPUT> based on a query is run once for every record that the query returns. If it returns no results, the code within the <CFOUTPUT> is never executed.

Notice the syntax of the condition in the above template. The condition is:

```
Getdetails.Recordcount LT 1
```

The LT here stands for less than. If you are used to programming in other languages this may be rather different, as less than is usually represented by the symbol <.

The following mnemonics are used in conditions within ColdFusion:

- **EQ** – equal to.
- **NEQ** – not equal to.
- **LT** – less than.
- **GT** – greater than.
- **LTE**– less than or equal to.
- **GTE** – greater than or equal to.

When you first start to program in ColdFusion you may find that you constantly forget about these mnemonics. Writing tests such as:

```
<CFIF Query.RecordCount = 0>
```

will reward you with an unhelpful error message such as:

```
Cannot add value to query
```

If you get strange error messages when writing <CFIF>s then it is always a good idea to check that you have used a mnemonic and not a symbol.

Branching again with <CFELSE>

<CFIF> runs the code inside itself if the condition specified is found to be true. You may want to run alternate code if this is false. <CFELSE> is used to separate the <CFIF> statement into code that is run if the condition

is true and code which is run if it is not. The <CFELSE> does not have a close tag, and can only be used inside a <CFIF>. It takes the following format:

```
<CFIF condition>
CFML and HTML ran if condition is true
<CFELSE>
CFML and HTML ran if condition it false
</CFIF>
```

This can be used for recursion, that is, a page can call itself. For instance, a *.cfm* template can check to see if a user is logged in (perhaps by checking a variable) and if so process their enquiry, and if not give their a message prompting them to log in. The following code gives an example of this. Save it in your *cftags* directory and call it *cfelse.cfm*:

```
<HTML>
<HEAD>
	<TITLE>CFELSE</TITLE>
</HEAD>
<BODY>
<CFIF isDefined("Form.password") AND Form.Password EQ "jamesbond">
	<H1>Greetings 007!</H1>
	<P>You have logged into the system
	<P>Please select a mission......
<CFELSE>
	You're not logged in!
	<FORM  method="post" action="cfelse.cfm">
	What is your password?
	<INPUT type="text" name="password">
	<INPUT type="SUBMIT" value="Login"
	</form>
</CFIF>
</BODY>
</HTML>
```

In the above example the template file uses <CFIF> to see if it has been posted a password from a form, and if so checks to see if the password is the valid one. If all is in order, the web page shows the relevant 'sensitive' data. If not it prompts the user to log in as shown in figure 8.3. You will notice that there are two conditions in the <CFIF>

joined together with an AND. This type of checking is explained in chapter 12.

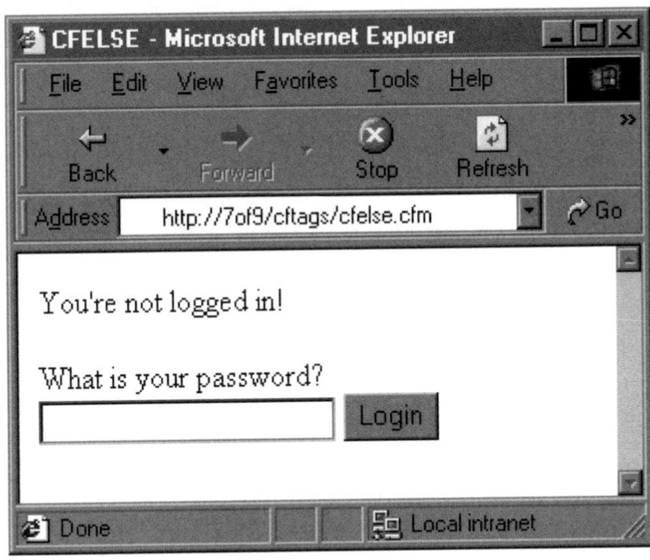

***Figure 8.3** – One view of our cfelse template file.*

At this point have a look at the source code of this page by selecting **View Source** from your browser. Notice that you get no clues from this page as to what the password is, or what the page will look like if you successfully log in. All you can see is the code to generate the form fields. The password and the sensitive data can only be viewed from the server by looking directly at the *.cfm* file. If you try to log in to the page several times using different incorrect passwords, you will notice that whatever you type, nothing changes until you type the correct password *jamesbond*, when you will be rewarded with the screen shown in figure 8.4. The <CFIF> group of tags enable a great deal of functionality to be built into very few template files. Have a look at the Crazy Cab email client demo that comes with ColdFusion to see how much functionality is possible with only a few template files.

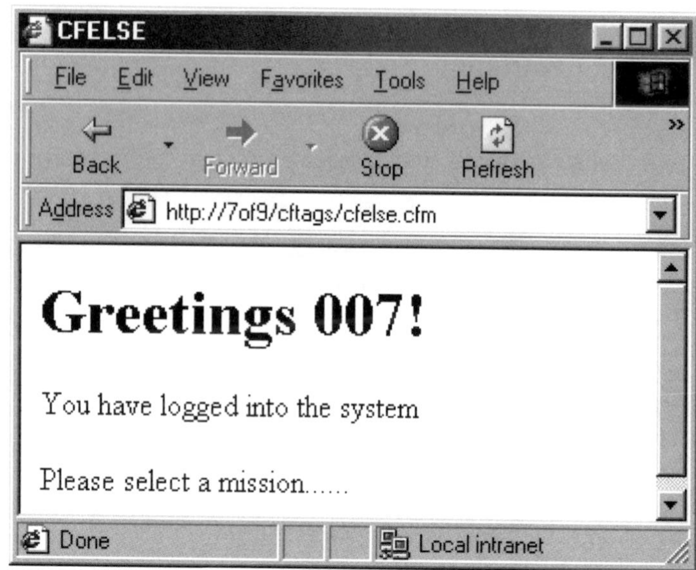

***Figure 8.4** – The cfif file when correctly logged in.*

<CFIF>s can be nested, or put inside each other, so even more complex branching can be carried out. A nested <CFIF> can take the following format:

```
<CFIF condition1>
      Action 1
<CFIF condition2>
      Action 2
</CFIF>
<CFELSE>
      <CFIF condition2>
            Action 3
      </CFIF>
</CFIF>
```

Multiple nested <CFIF>s can be confusing to program, and even more to debug, so when you are coding them try and use the tab key to format the <CFIF>s so that the start and end tags line up and everything that is triggered by the condition is indented. It is also important to comment your code, by writing comments to yourself within the code telling you what it does. A comment in CMFL is marked by the following 'tag':

```
<!--- Text of notes here --->
```

You can even put comment marks around pieces of code, which is sometimes useful for debugging. The ColdFusion server ignores anything within the comment tags, it switches off the commented code without deleting it from the template. This is useful if you are not entirely sure which part of your template is not working since it helps you to identify problem areas.

Branching again with <CFELSEIF>

This tag is used when you want to test for several conditions at once while still reserving the right to have a default operation if none of them are true. <CFELSEIF> is used after the <CFIF> but before the <CFELSE> as follows:

```
<CFIF condition1>
Action 1
<CFELSEIF>
Action 2
<CFELSEIF>
Action 2
<CFELSE>
Default Action
</CFIF>
```

We can demonstrate the use of this when referring to the number of records we get back from a search. Take the following statements that you may make after a search has been performed:

- Sorry your search found no records.
- Your search found one record.
- Your search found 100 records.

You will notice that there are three possible outcomes to any search that all have to be referred to differently, namely no records, one record, and many records. We can use the <CFELSEIF> to implement this type of response to our web queries as follows:

```
<HTML>
<HEAD>
	<TITLE>CFelseIf</TITLE>
</HEAD>
<BODY>
<CFQUERY datasource="MyLog" name="People">
	Select * from VisitorBook
	WHERE Name = 'Christopher Bowers'
</CFQUERY>
<H1>Here are our visitor book entries:</H1><BR>
<CFOUTPUT query="People"><BR>#ID#. #Name#</CFOUTPUT>
<BR>
<CFIF People.Recordcount EQ 0>
	Sorry! No one has signed our visitor book yet...
<CFELSEIF People.Recordcount EQ 1>
	One person has signed up so far.
<CFELSE>
<CFOUTPUT>#People.Recordcount# people have
signed our visitor book
</CFOUTPUT>
</CFIF>
</BODY>
</HTML>
```

Figure 8.5 shows what you would expect to see if you ran this through your browser.

To check the rest of your code we need to make a couple of changes. Comment out the **WHERE** clause by making it look as follows:

```
<!--- WHERE Name = 'Christopher Bowers' --->
```

Save the file and refresh your page. Figure 8.6 shows the new results, our summary of the files at the end of the listing uses the correct grammatical terms for the number we are referring to.

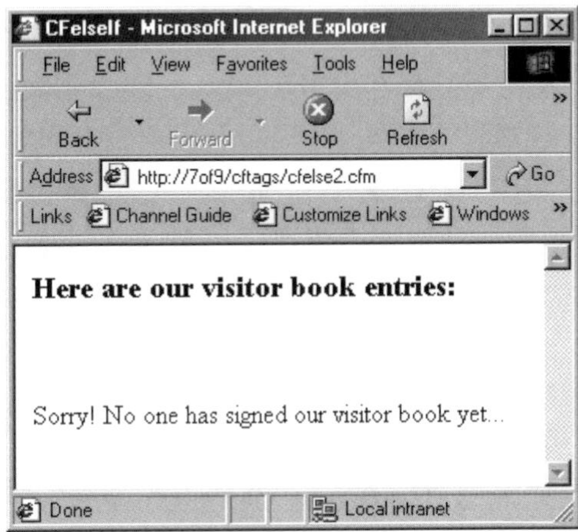

Figure 8.5 – *First <CFIF> result.*

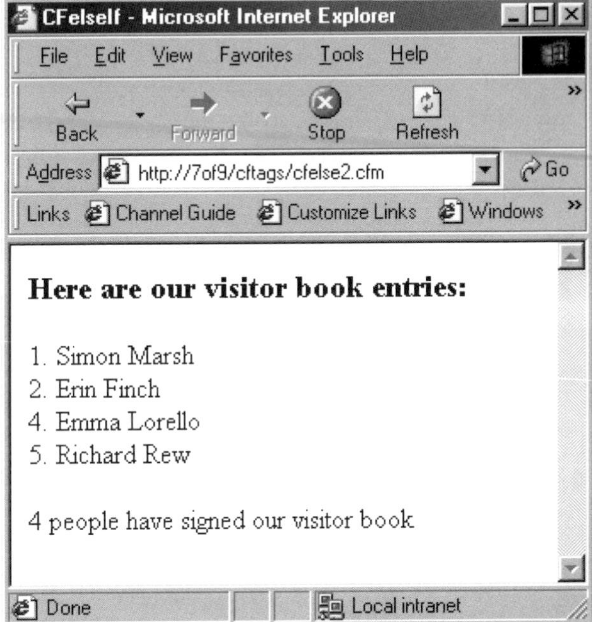

Figure 8.6 - *Second <CFELSEIF> result.*

Remove the comments around the WHERE clause and replace the name with a name that exists in your visitor book database; in our case we used:

```
WHERE Name = 'Erin Finch'
```

Figure 8.7 shows the results when our query returns just one hit, the text summary is displayed correctly.

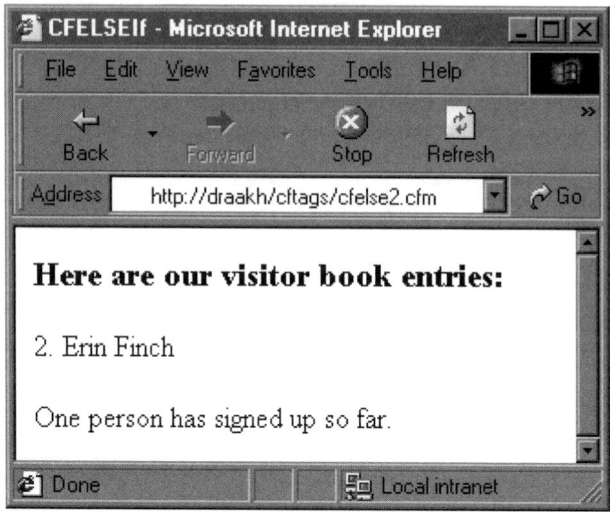

Figure 8.7 *– Third <CFELSE> result.*

<CFSWITCH>

Our previous example used several different <CFIF>, <CFELSEIF> and <CFELSE> tags to take an action depending on different results of a test. This is so frequently used in programming that ColdFusion has a special tag for this very purpose. It is used with the tags <CFCASE> and <CFDEFAULTCASE> formatted as follows:

```
<CFSWITCH expression="expression">
<CFCASE value="value" delimiters="delimiter">
    HTML and CFML to run
</CFCASE>
More <CFCASE></CFCASE>
<CFDEFAULTCASE>
    HTML and CFML to run
```

```
</CFDEFAULTCASE>
</CFSWITCH>
```

- **expression** is what you are testing. It could be anything that you are able to compare with something else, for example a numeric variable, text or a Boolean.
- **value** is the specific value that you are testing for at the time. This could be one value or a list of values. If you use a list you have to specify what character you are using in the **delimiters** attribute.

To see how <CFSWITCH> works here is the function we created in the previous <CFIF> example rewritten using <CFSWITCH>.

```
<HTML>
<HEAD>
	<TITLE>CFelseIf</TITLE>
</HEAD>
<BODY>
<CFQUERY datasource="MyLog" name="People">
Select * from VisitorBook
Where Name = 'Erin Finch'
</CFQUERY>
<H3>Here are our visitor book entries:</H3>
<CFOUTPUT query="People">#ID#. #Name#<BR></CFOUTPUT>
<BR>
<CFSWITCH EXPRESSION="People.Recordcount">
	<CFCASE VALUE="0">
		Sorry! No one has signed our visitor book yet...
	</CFCASE>
	<CFCASE VALUE="1">
		One person has signed up so far.
	</CFCASE>
	<CFDEFAULTCASE>
		<CFOUTPUT>#People.Recordcount# people have signed our
							visitor book</CFOUTPUT>
	</CFDEFAULTCASE>
</CFSWITCH>
</BODY>
</HTML>
```

Try running the above code in your browser again, changing and commenting out the **WHERE** clause to alter the query results and test all of your <CFSWITCH> branches.

Chapter

9

Email and the Internet

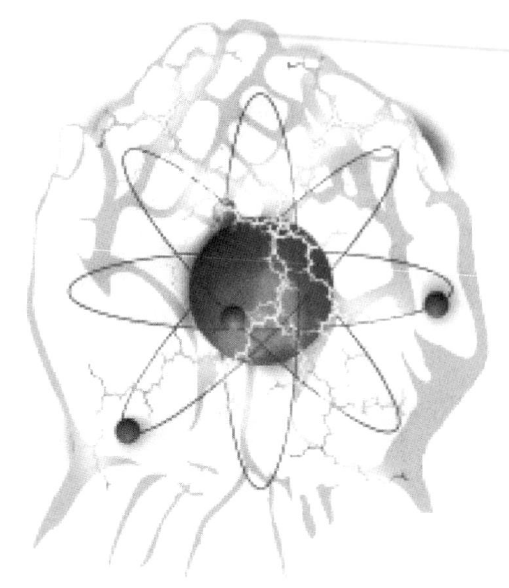

Introduction

As the main purpose of our use of ColdFusion is to write web applications for the Internet, at some stage it is likely that you are going to have to interact with other web technologies.

Allaire have provided several tags that enable the sending and receipt of email, and the downloading, processing and redirection of web pages. This chapter describes the following tags, which allow you to do this:

- <CFMAIL>
- <CFPOP>
- <CFHTTP>
- <CFLOCATION>

Mail Functions

ColdFusion provides the developer with tags that allow the manipulation of email on remote servers. The two tags are:

- **<CFMAIL>** Which is used for sending email through an SMTP mail gateway anywhere on the internet.
- **<CFPOP>** Which allows you to download emails from any email server that supports the POP3 protocol. The emails are returned as if they are the results of a <CFQUERY>.

To use the examples in this email section you will need details of your account on a POP3 server and details of an SMTP gateway that you are authorized to send emails through.

Sending mail with <CFMAIL>

There are times when you need your web server to send emails. ColdFusion has a tag designed to do this which can be very useful. <CFMAIL> takes the following format:

```
<CFMAIL to="RecipientEmail"
from="SendersEmail"
cc="CarbonCopyEmail"
subject="EmailSubject"
type="MessageType"
mimeattach="ServerPathtoFile"
query="Query"
maxrows="MaximumQueryRows"
group="GroupByQueryColumn"
startrow="FirstRowToUse"
server="SMTPServerName"
port="SMTPServerPort"
mailerid="MailHeaderID"
timeout="TimoutInSeconds">
Mail Message body
</CFMAIL>
```

- **to**, **from**, **cc** and **subject** are all standard email terms, and should be completed as if you are sending a normal email. You can also use a variable in any of those fields. If, for instance, you had the user's email stored in a variable called *UEMAIL,* you could use the attribute *From="#UEMAIL#"* to refer to their email. Interestingly, the **From** field can be any email address, which means that you can use this to send email on behalf of other people. Remember that you will need their permission to do this.
- **Type** refers to the type of email that you are sending. To send a plain text email this attribute can be omitted, however if you are sending an HTML email the type should be set to *HTML*. These are the only options implemented at the moment.
- **Mimeattach** is used if you wish to add an attachment to the email and should be the full path to the file on

the server. If ColdFusion is mounted on an NT box you will need to make sure that the ColdFusion and Web Server service have access rights to the file. It also should be smaller than the maximum file size for attachments permitted by your mail service.

- **Query**, **maxrows**, **group** and **startrows** are used if you wish to send an email out to every record returned by a query. The <CFMAIL> tag essentially becomes like a <CFOUTPUT> if these attributes are used. The attributes have the same function as they would in that tag. One of the fields returned by your query will need to contain an email address, which needs to be put in the **To** field. If this is the case the **Query** attribute must appear before the **To** attribute.
- **Server** is the SMTP mail server that you wish to use for sending the mail. If you are unsure of what to put here look in the properties of the program that you normally use to send mail. This field can be omitted if the Server is set in the ColdFusion Administrator.
- **Port** is the TCP/IP port that the mail server above is using to receive mail. Most mail servers use port 25 for this.
- **MailerID** – this puts a header in the email that is sent that tells the recipient what mail program was used to send the mail. If you are writing a custom mail application then you may wish to use that attribute. If you omit it then the header will contain the application *Allaire ColdFusion Application Server.*
- **Timeout** – this is the number of seconds that ColdFusion waits to connect to the server. If your mail server is not responding then ColdFusion will stop trying to send the email once this time is reached.
- **Mail Message Body** is the email message you wish to send. You are not limited to text here but can include ColdFusion functions tags and variables to create your email.

Although the above contains lots of attributes, <CFMAIL> can be used quickly and simply if you just want to send an email and know the mail server on your network.

Sending an email

For instance, if your development system is connected to the Internet, and your ISP mail server is *mail.isp.net* the following would send the author an email.

```
<HTML>
<HEAD>
      <TITLE>MailTest</TITLE>
</HEAD>
<BODY>
<CFMAIL TO="mnorman@dmu.ac.uk"
  FROM="person@readers.net"
  SUBJECT="Testing CFMAIL"
  SERVER="mail.isp.net"
PORT="25">
            Hi there,
            I'm a reader, and I'm just testing the CFMAIL function
            from your book
</CFMAIL>
</BODY>
</HTML>
```

Make sure the machine with ColdFusion on is connected to the Internet and run the above *.cfm* template file via a browser. You will be rewarded with a blank screen but hopefully you will have successfully sent an email using the server. Bear in mind that some mail servers do not allow you to send email through them if you are not a recognized user, so make sure you use a valid email address for the mail server you are forwarding the mail to. Try sending yourself an email to test it, remembering that you need to be connected to the Internet for it to work.

Failed email

Sending mail can be problematic. You could specify an incorrect email address or the server could be down. If you do not receive your email or think that there is a problem with sending to others look at the:

```
CFUSION/MAIL/UNDELIVR
```

directory on your ColdFusion server. This directory contains all failed mail messages, and should therefore be checked regularly to be aware of problems.

Sending emails to a group

The following code shows how you could use the query processing function of <CFMAIL> to send a message to all of the people who have signed your visitor book:

```
<HTML>
<HEAD>
	<TITLE>Mail by Query</TITLE>
</HEAD>
<BODY>
<CFQUERY datasource="MyLog" name="SendEmail" >
	Select Email,Name
	from VisitorBook
</CFQUERY>
<CFMAIL TO="#Email#"
  FROM="person@readers.net"
  SUBJECT="Testing CFMAIL By Group"
  SERVER="mail.isp.net"
	QUERY="SendEmail">
Hi there #Name#
Just wanted to say thankyou
for leaving a message on my visitor book
</CFMAIL>
</BODY>
</HTML>
```

Notice how you do not need to put <CFOUTPUT> around the #Name# field in the message text, as the whole tag acts as a <CFOUTPUT> anyway. If you have valid email addresses in your visitor book you may wish to save the above as a *.cfm* file and run it. You may have to change the text to explain to the recipients that you are using their addresses as a test.

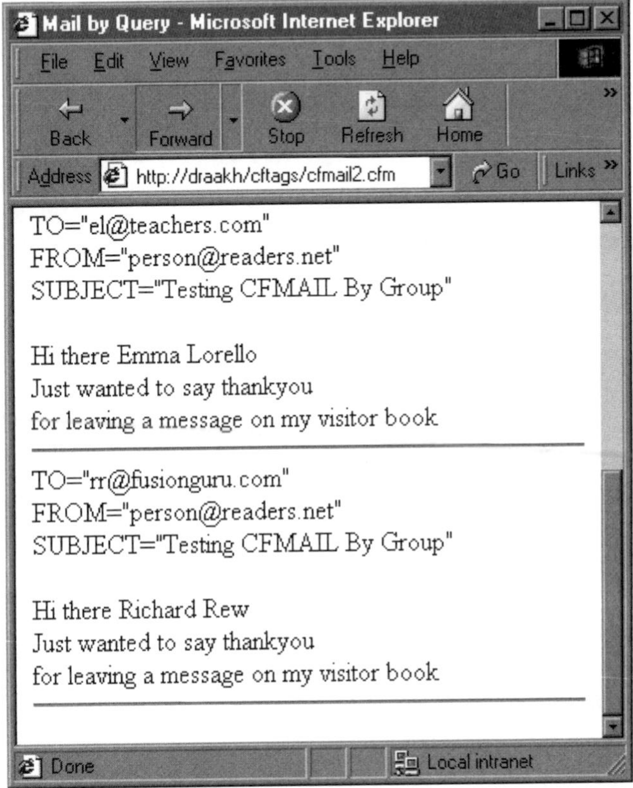

***Figure 9.1** – User feedback from a <CFMAIL> operation.*

Notice also that all you get when you run the *.cfm* file is a blank page, as <CFMAIL> does not generate any output via HTML. It is good practice to add a <CFOUTPUT> into the BODY of your template file that prints the email out as well so that you can check it looks as it should. You could do this by adding the following after the </CFMAIL> end tag:

```
<CFOUTPUT QUERY="SendEmail">
TO="#Email#"<BR>
FROM="person@readers.net"<BR>
SUBJECT="Testing CFMAIL By Group"<BR>
<BR>
Hi there #Name#<BR>
Just wanted to say thankyou <BR>
for leaving a message on my visitor book<BR>
<HR>
</CFOUTPUT>
```

This gives the user some positive feedback that the mail has been sent, part of which can be seen in figure 9.1.

Getting mail with <CFPOP>

Now we have learnt how to send mail via ColdFusion, we can discuss how to receive mail. ColdFusion can receive mail from mail servers on the Internet or your LAN that use Post Office Protocol (POP3) using <CFPOP>. When provided with a mail server and user details the ColdFusion server will access the mail on the mail server and return the results as if it was a query. You then use <CFOUTPUT> to get the email details back from the server. The <CFPOP> tag uses the following format:

```
<CFPOP SERVER="MailServerName"
  PORT="MailPortName"
  USERNAME="YourUsername"
  PASSWORD="YourPassword"
  ACTION="PopAction"
  NAME="NameOfQuery"
  MESSAGENUMBER="MessageID"
  ATTACHMENTPATH="ServerPathToSaveFiles"
  TIMEOUT="OperationTimeout"
  MAXROWS="MaximumRows"
  STARTROW="FirstRow">
```

- **Server** is the full domain name of your POP3 server on the Internet. As with <CFMAIL> if you are not sure of what your server is called look in the settings of the program that you usually use to send and receive mail.

- **Port** is the port that the mail server listens to. The default is usually port 110.
- **Username** and **Password** are the authorization credentials for your mail server.
- **Action** is what you want the POP3 operation to do. It can be one of three options:

    - GetHeaderOnly.
    - GetAll.
    - Delete.

  These will be explained in the next sections.
- **Name** identifies this POP query in CFOUTPUT tags to get the email details back later in your code.
- **Messagenumber** is the ID of the message that you are requesting. ColdFusion numbers each message that you download with CFPOP consecutively. You can then use this number to return to a message to manipulate it further. Your ColdFusion server itself assigns the message number, and it will continue to refer to that message with the same number until you send a delete command. As the **Delete** command could affect your numbering all numbering is reset after each **Delete** you issue.
- **Attachmentpath** is the path on the server where you want ColdFusion to store any attachments that it may find in the emails.
- **Timeout** is the time in seconds that ColdFusion will wait for the POP3 server to respond before it stops with an error.
- **Maxrows** and **startrows** have the same meaning as elsewhere in ColdFusion.

As you can see from the **action** attribute above there are three distinct ways that you can use <CFPOP>:

- First you download a list of the headers to your machine, taking note of the message ID of each header.

- Second, by specifying the message ID number, you download all of the information related to that single email, or all of the details for all of the emails.
- Finally, you delete the email you have just downloaded from the pop server (if required).

We will now demonstrate each of the above actions.

<CFPOP> GetHeaderOnly

The first operation that <CFPOP> does is to download the message headers. As this ignores the message body and any file attachments, it should be a fairly quick process. Use the following listing to create a template file that lists all of your headers:

```
<HTML>
<HEAD>
	<TITLE>CFPOP Get Headers</TITLE>
</HEAD>
<BODY>
<CFPOP SERVER="pop3.myisp.net"
 PORT="110"
 USERNAME="yourname"
 PASSWORD="yourpassword"
 ACTION="GETHEADERONLY"
 NAME="getmail" >
<CFOUTPUT query="getmail">
	#MESSAGENUMBER#. #From# #Subject#<HR>
</CFOUTPUT>
<CFOUTPUT>
	#getmail.Recordcount# messages downloaded
</CFOUTPUT>
</BODY>
</HTML>
```

Save the above code as *cfpop.cfm* and store it in your *cftags* directory making sure to include your POP3 server name and user credentials. It may be a good idea to send yourself an email before you run this template so that you have something to work with. Once you have sent the email look at *cfpop.cfm* with your browser. Figure 9.2 shows the results for one email.

***Figure 9.2** – Downloading message headers with <CFPOP>*

The example in the above template only refers to three of the field names that are available from the <CFPOP> query when used with GetHeaderOnly. The complete set of fields you can access in <CFOUTPUT> are:

- **MessageNumber.** This is the unique number that ColdFusion applies to the email until <CFPOP> is called with the Delete action. At that point ColdFusion will renumber its list of emails.
- **From.** The sender of the message.
- **Subject.** The subject of the message.
- **Date.** The date the email was sent.
- **ReplyTo.** The email address that the sender would like you to reply to.
- **CC.** Who else the email has been sent to as a carbon copy.
- **To.** Who the email has been sent to. This should be your email address.

<CFPOP> GetAll

Once you have used the *GetHeaderOnly* action to get the message ID of the email you wish to fully download, you can use the GetAll action of CFPOP to retrieve the full email. If you omit the **messagenumber** attribute from the tag, you will download all the email on the server. Save the following code as *cfpopall.cfm* and run it in your browser:

```
<HTML>
<HEAD>
    <TITLE>CFPOP Get All</TITLE>
</HEAD>
<BODY>
<CFPOP SERVER="pop3.myisp.net"
 PORT="110"
 USERNAME="yourname"
 PASSWORD="yourpassword"
 ACTION="GETALL"
 NAME="getmail"
 MESSAGENUMBER=1>
<CFOUTPUT query="getmail">#MESSAGENUMBER#.#From#
    #Subject#<BR>
    #Body#<HR>
</CFOUTPUT>
<CFOUTPUT>
    #getmail.Recordcount# messages downloaded
</CFOUTPUT>
</BODY>
</HTML>
```

The above code is shown in a browser window in figure 9.3. If it does not it may be that you have received more email since running *cfpop.cfm*. If this is the case rerun *cfpop.cfm* and alter *cfpopall.cfm* to point to the exact email you wish to download. If you do this quickly enough you should download the correct email. In a real system you would use forms and hyperlinks to select the email dynamically.

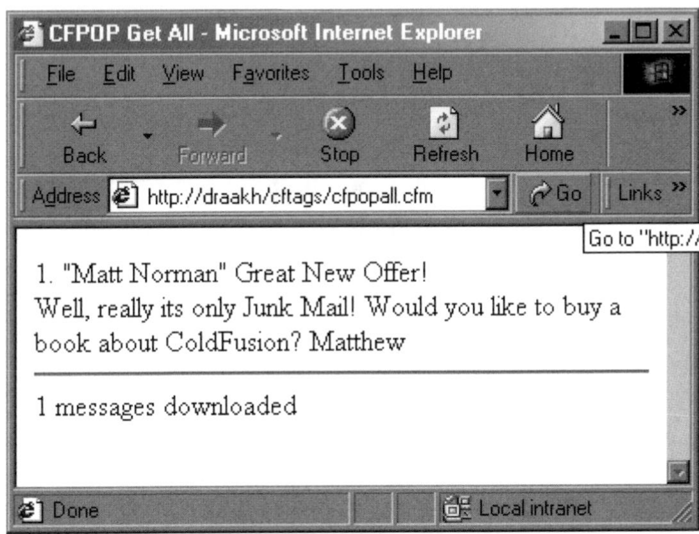

Figure 9.3 – Downloading full message with <CFPOP>.

Using GetAll <CFPOP> gives you the following extra field names to use in your <CFOUTPUT>:

- **Body.** This is the main text of the email, the actual message.
- **Header.** This contains the full header information about the email, all the details of how it got to you.

GetAll will also handle and download attachments as well but only if you tell ColdFusion where to place the attached files on the server with the **attachmentpath** attribute. If you use this you get two more column names to experiment with in your <CFOUTPUT> tag:

- **Attachments** which contains a list of the attached files, as several can be sent with one message. Tab is used to separate entries in this list.
- **Attachmentfiles.** As attachments could have the same filename, ColdFusion saves each attachment with a random name, which is stored in this list. Again this is separated with tabs. When you are writing your code to handle the attachments you will need to match these two lists together and copy the files elsewhere to do with them as you need.

<CFPOP> Delete

Once you have finally dealt with the email you can remove it from the server. You need to make sure that this is really what you want to do. If you are writing an application just to let users access their mail over the web as an addition to their normal email access then it may be an idea not to give them the opportunity to delete the mail as you cannot get it back once deleted. If your application is the only method your users have to get to their email then you need to implement a delete function. The following template shows how to delete the email that we have been looking at in the last few examples. Bear in mind that this will delete the first email on your pop server, so if you have not read it yet do not run this file.

```
<HTML>
<HEAD>
	<TITLE>Delete Message</TITLE>
</HEAD>
<BODY>
<CFPOP SERVER="pop3.myisp.net"
 PORT="110"
 USERNAME="yourname"
 PASSWORD="yourpassword"
 ACTION="DELETE"
 MESSAGENUMBER="1" >
<P>Message deleted
</BODY>
</HTML>
```

This POP action will not give you any feedback, and gives you no query output, so the name attribute is not necessary. Remember that the messages that are still on your pop server will now have renumbered themselves, so if you re-run the script it will delete a different email; unlike a standard email reader you will not be given an “Are you sure?” prompt.

Manipulating web pages

Sometimes you will need ColdFusion to get web pages for you so that you can process them in some way. For instance a search engine works by pulling a page back from a web server and processing the page, by storing links and other text in its database. It then uses the links to repeat the process, downloading more pages.

ColdFusion provides two tags to process web pages:

- **<CFHTTP>** – This downloads the whole content of the specified web page to a variable on the server. The page is downloaded as a text HTML file.
- **<CFLOCATION>** – This displays the contents of a web page as if the web page had been called directly.

These tags will now be described in greater detail.

Getting web pages - <CFHTTP>

You can get ColdFusion to download web pages using the <CFHTTP> tag as follows:

```
<CFHTTP url="WebAddress"
Port="WebServerPort"
Method="POST/GET"
Username="RemoteUserName"
Password="RemotePassword"
Path="PathOnServer"
File="FileToUpload">
```

- **Url** is the web address you wish to download. *Port* is optional and used if you want to access a port other than the standard http port which is 80.
- **Method** selects if you want to download (Get) or upload (Post) a file. If you are using Post you also have to use the <CFHTTPPARAM> tag to specify extra attributes for the Post. Further details of

<CFHTTPPARAM> are in *the CFML Language Reference Manuals.*

- **Username** and **password** are required if the remote system requires user authentication.
- **Path** is the location of the file that you wish to upload, or if you are downloading where to put the downloaded file. If you are downloading the file and do not specify a path, ColdFusion returns the file in the variable **FileContent.**
- **File** is only used if you are posting a file. It is the name of the file that you are uploading.

The following code uses <CFHTTP> to download a web page. It does not do any processing on the page, it just displays it:

```
<HTML>
<HEAD>
	<TITLE>CFHTTP</TITLE>
</HEAD>
<BODY>
<CFHTTP method="GET" url="www.google.com">
<P>Downloaded the following page:
<TABLE border=1><TR><TD>
<CFOUTPUT>#CFHTTP.FileContent#</CFOUTPUT>
</TD></TR></TABLE>
</BODY>
</HTML>
```

Figure 9.4 shows the results of the above when run on a ColdFusion server that is also connected to the Internet. The downloaded page has been placed into a table to highlight what has been downloaded. This example has limited use, but as you become more proficient at string handling functions you can download web pages from anywhere on the web to your server, strip out the relevant information and pass only the important information to your users.

Figure 9.4 – <CFHTTP> downloading from other web sites.

Moving elsewhere <CFLOCATION>

<CFLOCATION> forces the ColdFusion Server to stop what it is processing in a template file and divert the user to another web location elsewhere. This is useful when you are branching using <CFIF> since sometimes you may

wish the template to move to a new page. <CFLOCATION> takes the following format:

```
<CFLOCATION URL="WebAddress"
ADDTOKEN="Yes/No">
```

- The **URL** attribute specifies where you want the server to redirect you web access to.
- The **AddToken** attribute is optional and is used to pass on variables that are used in the current template via the URL to the next page or template.

If the page that you want to redirect to is not on your ColdFusion server, you need to remember to put *http://* in front of the web address. If this is omitted you will probably get an *HTTP 500 Server Error* message.

To demonstrate, the following script redirects the user to another web site, but before it does that it logs the fact.

```
<HTML>
<HEAD>
	<TITLE>CFLOCATION</TITLE>
</HEAD>
<BODY>
<CFQUERY datasource="MyLog" name="LogThem">
Insert into Log(AccessDateAndTime,PageName,HostIPNum,Browser)
Values ( #Now()#, 'Off to Easyrew', '#CGI.REMOTE_HOST#', '#CGI.HTTP_USER_AGENT#' )
</CFQUERY>
<CFLOCATION url="http://www.easyrew.com?ecf">
<P>Whatever is here won't get processed!
</BODY>
</HTML>
```

Figure 9.5 shows the output of the above template file when saved as *cflocation.cfm*. Notice the URL of the web page in this figure. Although the page is an external page the actual address is still of the template file on your server. You could use template files like this to log accesses to external sites from your site. Instead of linking directly to www.easyrew.com through the following tag:

```
<A href="http://www.easyrew.com?ecf">Go to EasyRew</A>
```

You can call your own template file instead as follows:

```
<A href="cflocation.cfm">Go to EasyRew</A>
```

You can then modify the *cflocation.cfm* template file so that you can log accesses to any external site and not just to the one hard coded into that template.

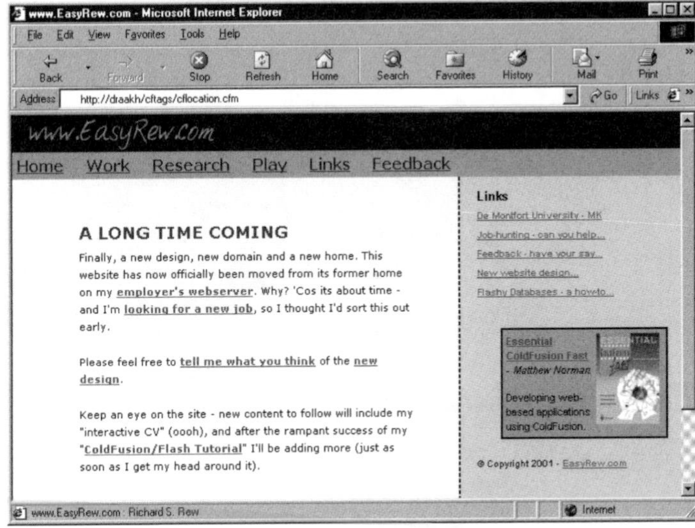

Figure 9.5 – <CFLOCATION> redirecting to a web page.

Chapter

10

CF Tags – File Functions

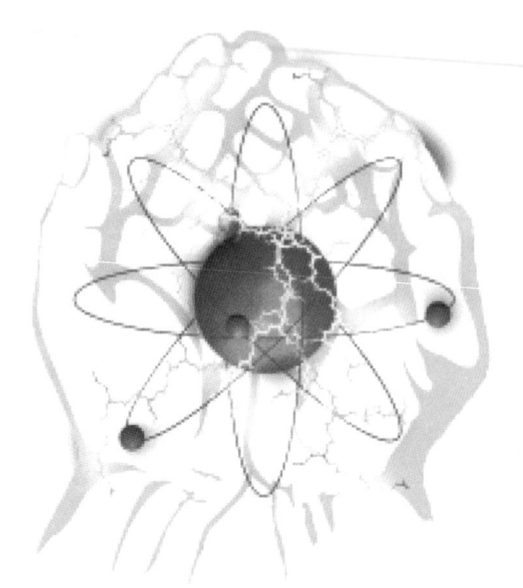

Introduction

Our ColdFusion server is running on a machine which itself is a file server. At some point we are going to need to manipulate the files on the server, whether it is just to list them remotely or to upload files or move and delete them.

Allaire have included some tags that handle file operations. This chapter describes two of them:

- <CFDIRECTORY> which is used to list the contents of a directory on your file server, as well as create and delete directories.
- <CFFILE> which can be used to copy, move, create delete and upload files.

Choose carefully whether or not to use, or allow the use of these tags on your web server. In the wrong hands these tags could seriously compromise your security, even rendering your servers useless.

First we describe the process of moving through our file server's file system by viewing directories.

Reading with <CFDIRECTORY>

<CFDIRECTORY> allows you to perform operations with directories on the ColdFusion server. <CFDIRECTORY> can be used to read the contents of, create, rename and delete directories. As this has security implications it can be turned off using the ColdFusion Administration. The tag takes the following format:

```
<CFDIRECTORY ACTION="directory action"
  DIRECTORY="directory name"
  NAME="query name"
  FILTER="list filter"
  MODE="permission"
  SORT="sort specification"
  NEWDIRECTORY="new directory name">
```

Action specifies what you want the tag to do. The action can be one of the following:

- List.
- Create.
- Rename.
- Delete.

If **Action** is omitted then <CFDIRECTORY> defaults to the list action which gathers the contents of the directory and gets it ready to output through a <CFOUTPUT> tag as follows:

```
<HTML>
<HEAD>
	<TITLE>Simple Directory</TITLE>
</HEAD>
<BODY>
<CFDIRECTORY directory="c:\inetpub"
	name="listdir">
<TABLE>
	<CFOUTPUT query="listdir">
		<TR>
			<TD>#Name# </TD>
			<TD>#Size# </TD>
			<TD>#Type# </TD>
			<TD>#DateLastModified# </TD>
			<TD>#Attributes#</TD>
		</TR>
	</CFOUTPUT>
</TABLE>
</BODY>
</HTML>
```

Figure 10.1 shows the above script if run on the web server when saved as *cfdir.cfm*. Notice how it contains most of the information that you would expect from a directory listing.

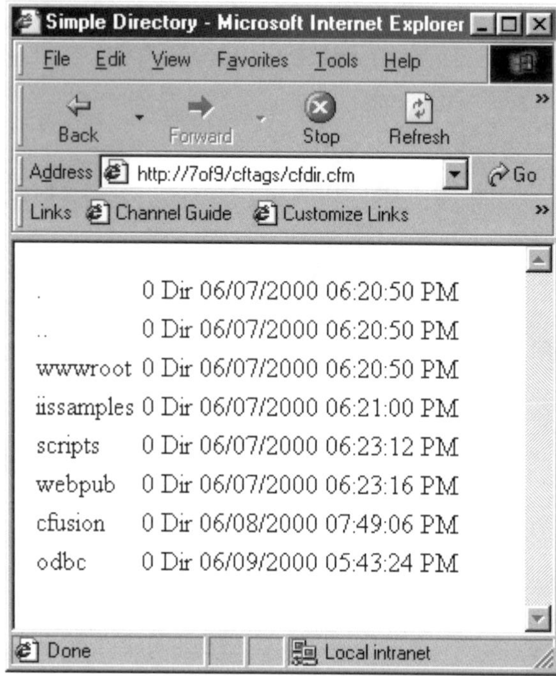

***Figure 10.1** – <CFDIRECTORY> of web server.*

To create a new directory we need to amend the tag description as follows:

```
<HTML>
<HEAD>
      <TITLE>Directory creation</TITLE>
</HEAD>
<BODY>
<CFDIRECTORY directory="c:\inetpub\testdir1"
      action="CREATE" >
<P>Directory testdir1 created!
<P><A href="cfdir.cfm">Click here to see!</A>
</BODY>
</HTML>
```

Save the above file as *cfdir2.cfm* and run it. There is a link that you can click on to check that the directory has been created by running *cfdir.cfm* again. Note that the new directory is specified in the directory attribute and *not* in the *newdirectory* attribute. Now we can rename the directory that you have just created. Alter the <CFDIRECTORY> tag in *cfdir2.cfm* to read as follows:

```
<CFDIRECTORY directory="c:\inetpub\testdir1"
        action="Rename"
        newdirectory="testdir2">
```

Save and run the file and when you rerun *cfdir.cfm* you will see that the directory has been renamed. To delete the directory amend *cfdir2* again so that the <CFDIRECTORY> tag reads as follows:

```
<CFDIRECTORY directory="c:\inetpub\testdir2"
        action="DELETE" >
```

As always, you can substitute many of the attributes with variables. As you have been running through the last few examples you may have experienced errors if you re-ran some of the scripts and ColdFusion could not find the correct directory. This will happen if you tried the rename and delete actions twice, as in both cases you will be referring to a directory that has either changed or already gone. If you want to create robust sites, use <CFIF> to check that the directory exists before referring to it.

File actions with <CFFILE>

Once we have created a directory, we can put files in it. The <CFFILE> tag is used to handle all file operations on the server. This could have security implications so there is the option to turn off this tag in ColdFusion Administrator. <CFFILE> has several actions that it can perform as follows:

- Upload.
- Move.
- Rename.
- Copy.
- Delete.
- Read.
- Write.
- Amend.

The *CFML Language Reference Manual* explains these in detail. Each action has its own specific set of attributes to use. For instance, **Upload** has the following format:

```
<CFFILE ACTION="Upload"
FILEFIELD="FieldName"
DESTINATION="directory"
NAMECONFLICT="action"
      ACCEPT="typeoffile" >
```

- **Upload** is used to accept files that have been uploaded to the server via a field name, **filefield**, in a form.
- **NameConflict** alerts ColdFusion of what to do when the file that you are writing to the server already exists. You can use either:
  - **Error.** This generates a *File Exists* error which gets passed back to the user. If you omit **NameConflict** this is the default action.
  - **Skip.** This file is not overwritten but no error is generated.
  - **Overwrite.** The old file is overwritten.
  - **MakeUnique.** The new file is saved with a new filename. If you are using a database to keep track of the filenames then you can access the filename that ColdFusion has made up for you through the variable ServerFile. Remember that this needs to be done soon after the <CFFILE> command as once you have moved to another template the name will be lost.
- **Accept** allows you to specify what type of file you are expecting, by means of specifying the MIME type of the file.

Another useful <CFFILE> action is *Write*, which can create a textfile on the server. This takes the following format:

```
<CFFILE ACTION="Write"
FILE="pathandname"
OUTPUT="WhatsInTheFile">
```

Once you have created the text file you can add lines to it by using the following:

```
<CFFILE ACTION="Append"
FILE="pathandname"
OUTPUT="WhatToAddToTheFile">
```

These two actions are very useful for generating log files for your website. If you do not need database functions on log files it is sometimes easier to write a transaction log out to a text file. To write an entry to the log file:

- First check to see if your log file exists using <CFIF>.
  - If it does not exist, then create a new file with the log entry.
  - If it does exist, then just append your entry into the file.

For more information about other <CFFILE> tag actions consult the *CFML Language Reference Manual.*

Chapter

11

Using ColdFusion Variables

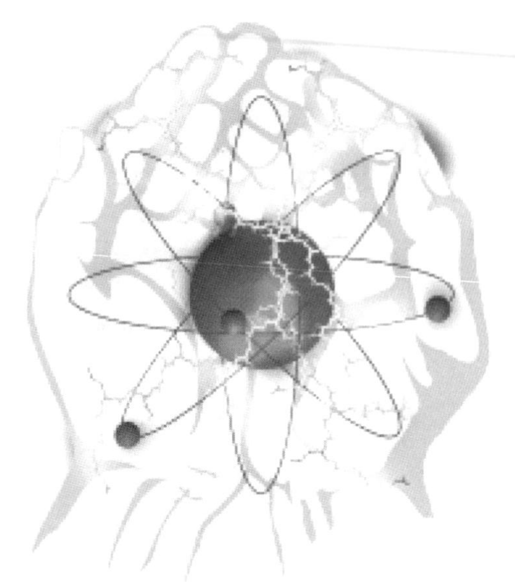

Introduction

Variables are an integral part of most programs, as they provide a place to store any data or information gleaned from the user to use to customize their experience. For instance, we could define a variable called *name*, and put the user's name in it. Then, throughout the course of the user's visit we can use that variable to make the name appear on every screen they visit. Once the user has finished we write the contents of the variable name to a database, which stores their name for future reference. The next time they arrive their name is retrieved and the user will be pleased to find his pages are personalized with his name.

There are many different types of variables in ColdFusion. This chapter will list the more common and describe how they are defined and used.

Query Variables

If you have been working your way through this book you will by now have used query variables. They are the method that you use to access the results of your query through <CFOUTPUT>. For instance, if you have a query that lists entries in our visitor book:

```
<CFQUERY datasource="MyLog" name="ListEntries">
Select *
from VisitorBook
</CFQUERY>
```

Every column name becomes a query variable. In the above example this leads to variables called:

- Name.
- Email.
- Comment.

- DateAndTime.
- Location.
- LikeSite.
- ID.

All of these variables can be referenced inside a <CFOUTPUT> by putting hashes (#) around the variable name. If you had several queries which used the same column names the individual variables can be referenced by putting the query name in front of the column name. For instance, in our query above, called *ListEntries*, the column *Email* could be uniquely referred to as:

```
#ListEntries.Email#
```

This prevents confusion between the same column names referenced by different queries.

Local Variables

Local variables are ones created with the <CFSET> command. They are only used within the particular template file that the user is accessing and only on that particular access. If the user clicks on a link to another template file the local variables will not be passed to the new template. <CFSET> has the following format:

```
<CFSET Variablename=value>
```

The variable is then referenced in a <CFOUTPUT> or inside another ColdFusion tag by putting hashes around it as usual. The following template file demonstrates a local variable called *tax*. Save this file as *tax.cfm* in a directory called *cffunctions* in your web server's *wwwroot* directory.

```
<HTML>
<HEAD>
	<TITLE>Local Variables</TITLE>
</HEAD>
<BODY>
<CFSET tax=17.5>
<CFOUTPUT>
```

```
        <BR>The basic rate of sales tax is #tax# %.
        <BR>Therefore everything that you buy has
        <BR>#tax# % of its value added back onto it.
        <BR>So if you were to buy a car that cost &pound;10000
        <BR>you would have to pay an extra
        &pound;#Evaluate(10000/100*tax)# in tax.
        <CFSET tax=tax*2>
        <BR>If the rate was doubled to #tax# %,
        <BR>then you would pay an extra
        &pound;#Evaluate(10000/100*tax)# in tax!
</CFOUTPUT>
</BODY>
</HTML>
```

Load the above template into your web browser. Figure 11.1 shows the results.

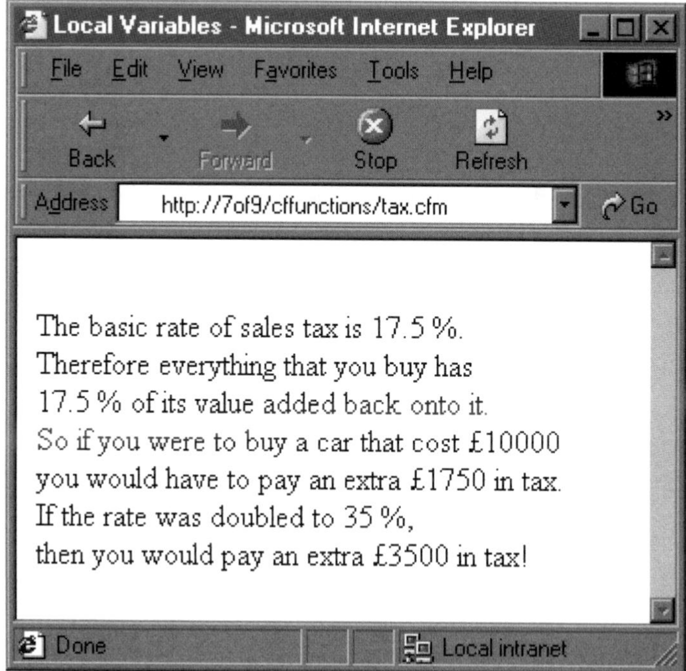

***Figure 11.1** – Using a local variable.*

Notice how that if the tax rate changes, all we have to do is change the <CFSET> variable and pay more tax! The rest of the document reflects the changes, as we have referenced the variable and not the value in it throughout. Try changing the value and refreshing the page to see how easy it becomes.

You will also notice that half way down the file, we multiply the contents of the variable by two, and store the new value back in the tax variable. Every reference after the change reflects that change.

Evaluate() is a function that causes ColdFusion to work out the calculation inside it. If you omitted this the calculation would just be printed on the web page and not the results of the calculation. Try replacing:

```
#Evaluate(10000/100*tax)#
```

with:

```
10000/100*#tax#
```

and you will see why it is needed.

URL Variables

Values can be passed to a template file through the URL. These can then be referenced in the template file by using the format:

```
#URL.variablename#
```

We can modify our previous template file to obtain the tax rate through the URL. Change the first <CFSET> to the following:

```
<CFSET tax=URL.taxrate>
```

Save the file as *url.cfm.* We then need to call the template file with a web browser, not forgetting to send the variable in via the URL. Do this by typing in the following URL:

```
http://WebServerName/cffunctions/url.cfm?taxrate=17.5
```

The results will be the same as figure 7.1, however this time we can check to see how much tax we have to pay on the car if the rate changes simply by editing the URL. You can add several variables to a URL by separating them with an ampersand as follows:

```
http://WebServerName/cffunctions/url.cfm?taxrate=17.5&carcost=10000
```

With the above information see if you can modify *url.cfm* to accept a changeable car cost as well. Also experiment with what happens if you omit the URL variables from the URL.

Normally you would not give people a URL with variables tagged on the end. However, they are more useful if embedded into a web link on a page, as the user just follows the link which has the variables already typed in for them. You should also avoid sending sensitive data, like login name and password, via a URL variable. These can easily be read from the screen and can be book marked which may represent a security risk.

If an HTTP form is used with the **method** attribute set to **get**, the form when submitted automatically appends all of the form fields on to the end of the URL as URL variables. This is another way to add URL variables but is again a possible security risk.

Form Variables

The most common way of getting information back from the user is by means of a form field. If the form uses the POST method, the template file that the form calls can access the variables using the format:

```
#FORM.formfieldname#
```

The following template file contains a form to get some of the visitor book data from the user. Save this file as *visitor.cfm* in your *cffunctions* directory.

```
<HTML>
<HEAD>
	<TITLE>Visitor Book</TITLE>
</HEAD>
<BODY>
```

```
<H2>Visitor Book</H2>
<TABLE>
<CFFORM action="logentry.cfm" method="POST">
<TR><TD>Your Name:</TD>
<TD><cfinput type="Text" name="VisitorName"></TD></TR>
<TR><TD>Your Home Town</TD>
<TD><cfinput type="Text" name="Location"></TD></TR>
<TR><TD>Your Email Address</TD>
<TD><cfinput type="Text" name="Email"></TD></TR>
<TR><TD>Your Comments</TD>
<TD><cfinput type="Text" name="Comments"></TD></TR>
<TR><TD><INPUT type="Submit" value="Submit"></TD></TR>
</CFFORM>
</TABLE>
</BODY>
</HTML>
```

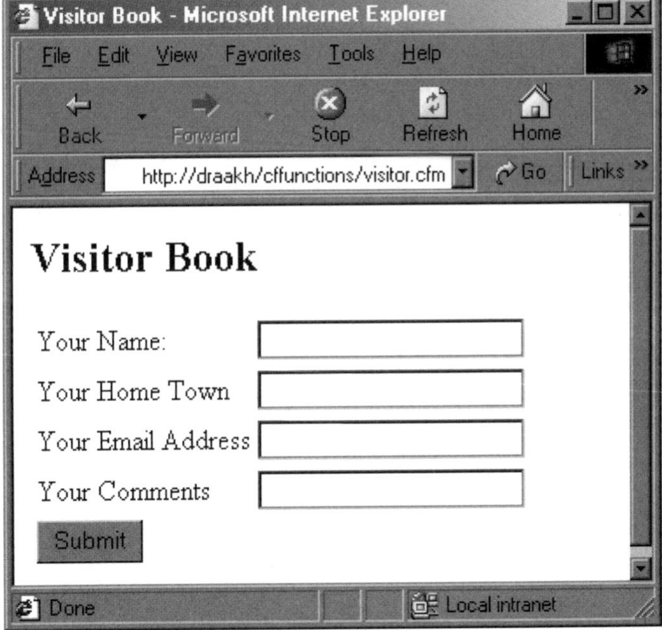

***Figure 11.2** – Form to submit form variables to visitor book.*

When the above template file is viewed through the browser it will look like figure 11.2. Before you enter data and submit the form we need to write the *logentry.cfm* to store and display the form variables as follows:

```
<HTML>
<HEAD>
<TITLE>Visitor Book Updated</TITLE>
</HEAD>
<BODY>
<CFQUERY datasource="MyLog" name="AddEntry">
Insert into VisitorBook(Name,Location,email,comment,DateAndTime)
Values('#Form.VisitorName#','#Form.Location#','#Form.email#',
'#Form.Comments#',#Now()#)
</CFQUERY>
<TABLE>
<TR><TD>Your Name:</td>
<TD><CFOUTPUT>#Form.VisitorName#</CFOUTPUT></td></tr>
<TR><TD>Your Home Town</td>
<TD><CFOUTPUT>#Form.Location#</CFOUTPUT></td></tr>
<TR><TD>Your Email Address</td>
<TD><CFOUTPUT>#Form.Email#</CFOUTPUT></td></tr>
<TR><TD>Your Comments</td>
<TD><CFOUTPUT>#Form.Comments#</CFOUTPUT></td></tr>
</table>
</BODY>
</HTML>
```

When you click on the submit button on the web page shown in figure 11.2 the above code is executed. Each form field from the previous template then becomes an active variable in the new template. The variable names are as follows:

- Form.VisitorName.
- Form.Location.
- Form.Email.
- Form.Comments.

We can do whatever calculations and manipulations that we want with these variables, but on this occasion we use them to drop a new record into our visitor book database. As that query provides no HTML output it is good practice to let the user know what they have just done, so the table after the query lets them know what they have just entered.

In practice, we would need to place links on this page to get them back to what they were doing before they clicked on the visitor book link.

Server Variables

These are variables that are available to all of the templates in use on a whole server. They are set using the following format:

```
<CFSET Server.Variablename=Value>
```

and are referred to within ColdFusion tags and <CFOUTPUT> by:

```
server.variablename
```

Once you run a template file that contains a server variable CFSET the variable will remain available to all other template files on that server until the ColdFusion service is stopped. This is useful for setting specific information about the server or the pages that are hosted on it. For instance, you may want to set the tax rate that we described earlier as a server variable if you are going to refer to it a lot and it changed infrequently. You have to remember though that these variables do need to be set when the server starts up if they are used throughout the system. The following template file saved as *server.cfm* sets a server variable and displays it and also displays some of the built in variables that are available to you:

```
<HTML>
<HEAD>
	<TITLE>Server Variables</TITLE>
</HEAD>
<BODY>
<CFSET server.ultimateanswer=42>
<CFOUTPUT>
	ProductName: #server.coldfusion.ProductName#<BR>
	ProductLevel: #server.coldfusion.ProductLevel#<BR>
	OS Name: #server.OS.name#<BR>
	OurVariable: #server.ultimateanswer#<BR>
```

```
</CFOUTPUT>
</BODY>
</HTML>
```

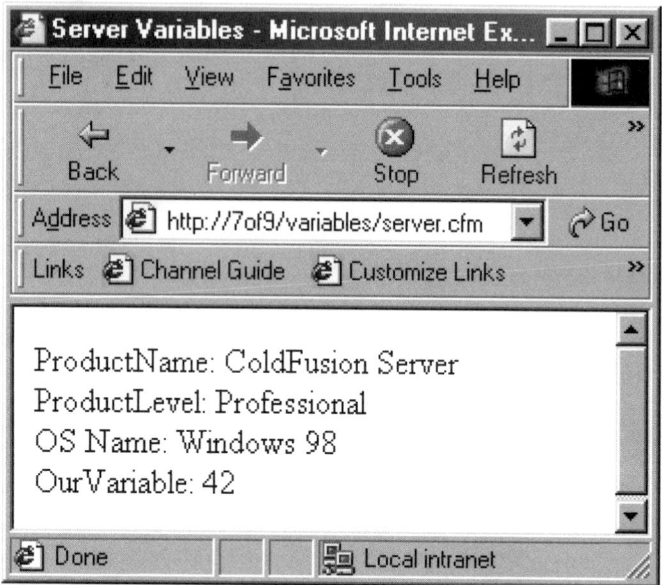

***Figure 11.3** – Built in server variables.*

Figure 11.3 shows the above file when displayed in a browser. To prove that the server variable we have set up is available to other template files figure 11.4 shows the following template file saved as *server2.cfm* displaying our saved value:

```
<HTML>
<HEAD>
    <TITLE>Server Variables 2</TITLE>
</HEAD>
<BODY>
<CFOUTPUT>
    OurVariable: #server.ultimateanswer#
</CFOUTPUT>
</BODY>
</HTML>
```

Other built-in server variables are described in the ColdFusion reference manuals.

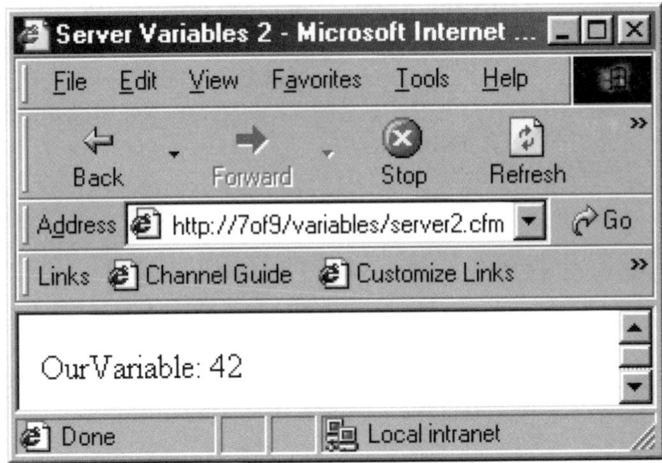

Figure 11.4 – Server variable from another template file.

CGI Environment variables

CGI environment variables are similar to server variables in that they are available to all template files on a server. They differ in that they are not user definable and are generated when a browser requests a page from the server. These variables are often described as CGI variables as they are available not just to ColdFusion scripts but any other CGI script running on the server. These variables give the developer some insight into the type of system that is viewing the page. If you have been following through this book we have used several CGI environment variables already in our page counter access logging mechanism.

For example in chapter 3 we used the following query to log a page access:

```
<CFQUERY name="addhit" datasource="MyLog">
Insert into Log (AccessDateAndTime,PageName,HostIPNum)
```

```
Values (#Now()#,'HomePage','#CGI.REMOTE_HOST#')
</CFQUERY>
```

In the above piece of code the IP number or domain name of the viewing web browser was stored into our database by using the CGI variable CGI.REMOTE_HOST. Consult the *ColdFusion Reference Manual* for a full list of CGI variables.

Cookies

Cookies are special sets of data that are stored on the machine that views the web pages. To set a cookie variable you use the <CFCOOKIE>tag as follows:

```
<CFCOOKIE Name="CookieName"
Value="CookieValue"
domain=".DomainName"
Expires="Expirytime">
```

- **Name** is the name under which the cookie is stored.
- **Value** is what you want to store.
- **DomainName** is the domain that you wish the cookie to be stored under.
- **Expires** sets the time that you want the cookie to expire. If you set this to Now the cookie is essentially deleted from the browser. If you set it to Never the cookie is permanent (until deleted explicitly). You can also set an expiry date for the cookie, or a number of days. If you don't specify an expiry time the cookie stays alive until the browser is exited.

When a browser looks at a page that sets a cookie, the cookie gets logged in the browser memory by storing it under the web site's domain name. When the browser is turned off the cookie is written to the disk of the client machine unless it has expired. You can see how many cookies you have by finding these files on your hard drive by looking for the domain names that you visit Figure 11.5

shows a small selection of cookie files found in my *Windows* directory that have been created by Internet Explorer.

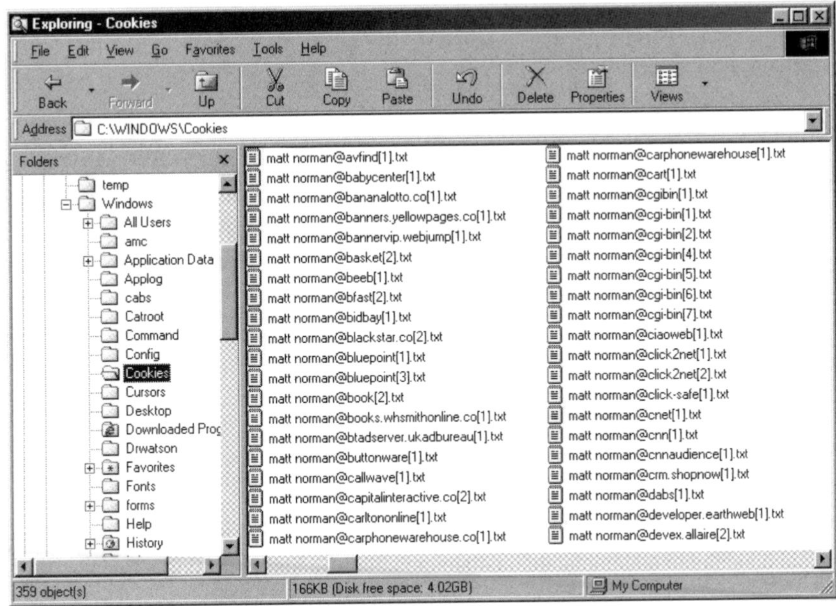

Figure 11.5 – Some Microsoft Internet Explorer cookies.

Because there is a possible security risk by storing cookies on remote machines, users can turn off the use of cookies in their browser settings. With this in mind you should not make your web site dependent on cookies. If you do, your first page should make the user aware that they need cookies enabled to use the site.

You should also be aware that a different cookie will be set for a different domain name. For example, your development machine will have a unique name that you call to access its web pages. In this book you may have noticed that I have used two different development machines to serve the ColdFusion code, namely *7of9* and *draakh*. When viewing these pages we could have called them in several different ways, for instance draakh's web pages can be called in the following ways:

- *http://draakh/*

- *http://draakh.coldfusionfast.com/*
- *http://146.227.132.129/*

Each of these methods is a valid way of calling a web server on a local area network. If you used each of these ways of calling the same template file, which set a cookie, this would result in *three separate cookie files* being saved on your local machine.

You can constrain this inconsistency by adding the **domain** attribute to the <CFCOOKIE> tag. This forces the cookie to be set to a specific domain rather than the domain that it was accessed by. The domain specified must always begin with a leading period. So if we were setting the cookie *username* on the *draakh* server we would use the following code:

```
<CFCOOKIE Name="username"
Value="matthew"
domain=".draakh.mk2.dmu.ac.uk">
```

The above code would force all cookies to be written to the draakh.mk2.dmu.ac.uk cookie file irrespective of the way that the user has called the web server.

One of the most useful uses of cookies is tracking a user's use of your site through several different visits, for instance to see if they continually come back to your site on repeated occasions. A mechanism to allow this tracking will be coded in chapter 14, but for now here are the steps needed to accomplish this:

- Add an extra column, called cookies, to your log database.
- Create a new table called cookies with an ID field that uses AutoNumber.
- In your accesslog code, check to see if the user has a cookie for your site.
    - If so, find the cookie value and write it to your access log.
    - If not, insert a new record into your cookies table. Retrieve this record to get its unique ID (from its AutoNumber field). Set a new cookie on the client machine using this number.

This method will not be foolproof in all occasions, but it is a valid way of seeing if people are returning to your site.

Other Variables

The above variables are not the only ones available to you as a ColdFusion programmer, however they are the ones that the author has used the most and found most useful. Other variable types are:

- *Client variables,* which ColdFusion assigns to a specific browser, and can be likened in a way to cookies.
- *Session variables,* which again are associated with a specific browser but are stored in the server's memory and expire when the browser stops viewing sites in a predefined period.
- *Application variables.* These are used within a ColdFusion application, and will be explained further in chapter 14.

Chapter

12

ColdFusion Functions

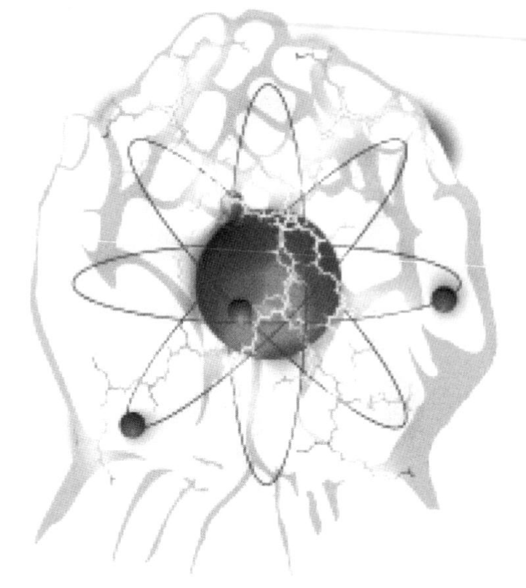

Introduction

A function is a pre-written piece of code that performs some kind of calculation or manipulation on data and returns a value or other data back to the main program.

At the last count ColdFusion had over 200 functions, however like many programming languages you will find that you regularly use only a few of them. With this in mind this chapter will only describe those functions that you will probably use as a web developer. If you want to learn how to use all of the functions then the CMFL Language Reference Manual is a well-written guide, but for an introduction to the more common or useful functions read on.

Check it is there with IsDefined

The **IsDefined** function checks to see whether a variable or parameter exists. This is a useful way of making sure that something exists before trying to use it. For example, the following template has a link in it that calls itself:

```
<HTML>
<HEAD>
	<TITLE>IsDefined</TITLE>
</HEAD>
<BODY>
<CFIF IsDefined("URL.rerun")>
This is the second time so there will be no link!
<CFELSE>
This is the first run of the template, so...<BR>
<A href="isdefined.cfm?rerun=yes">Please Click Here</A>
</CFIF>
</BODY>
</HTML>
```

Save the above as *isdefined.cfm* for it to work correctly. The first time the template runs it uses *IsDefined()* to check if there is a URL attribute. As there will not be, it runs the code that provides the URL to click on. Clicking on this link calls the page again, this time with a URL parameter. The second time it runs, it sees that the URL is defined and so displays the other web page. Figure 12.1 shows this behaviour. Notice that we never use the value that is stored in rerun. The rerun variable is purely being used as a flag in this case. If it is there, then we do one thing, if it is not, we do another.

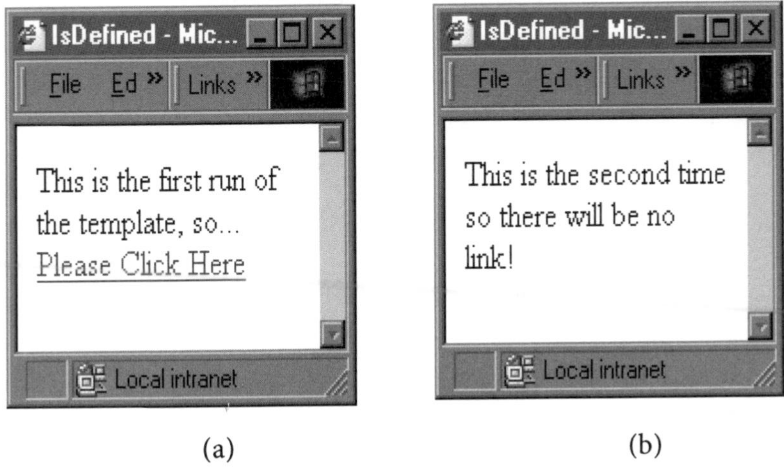

Figure 12.1 *– Different behaviour for the same template.*

If you were just to check if the URL parameter contained a value, and there was no URL parameter, then the template would stop with a 'variable not found' error. The **IsDefined** function prevents this error occurring and therefore allows web pages to function more reliably. A brief discussion with colleagues revealed that this is one of the most commonly used function in ColdFusion.

Check for a file – FileExists

This function is similar to **IsDefined** in that it checks for the existence of something, in this case a file on the server. This function takes the format:

```
Fileexists("PathAndFilename")
```

It returns true if the file is there and false if it is not. **FileExists** is useful if you are about to write a new file to the server. If you fail to check that the file is there and try and create a new one, if the file already exists ColdFusion returns an error to the user. The following template demonstrates the use of the **FileExists** function:

```
<HTML>
<HEAD>
    <TITLE>FileExists</TITLE>
</HEAD>
<BODY>
    <CFSET TheFile="C:\autoexec.bat">
    <CFIF FileExists(TheFile)>
        <P>The <CFOUTPUT>#TheFile#</CFOUTPUT>
            files exists on this machine
    <CFELSE>
        <P>This machine has no
            <CFOUTPUT>#TheFile#</CFOUTPUT> file
    </cfif>
</BODY>
</HTML>
```

Figure 12.2 shows that the machine *draakh* has an autoexec.bat file. Notice how the function will accept a variable, in this case *TheFile*.

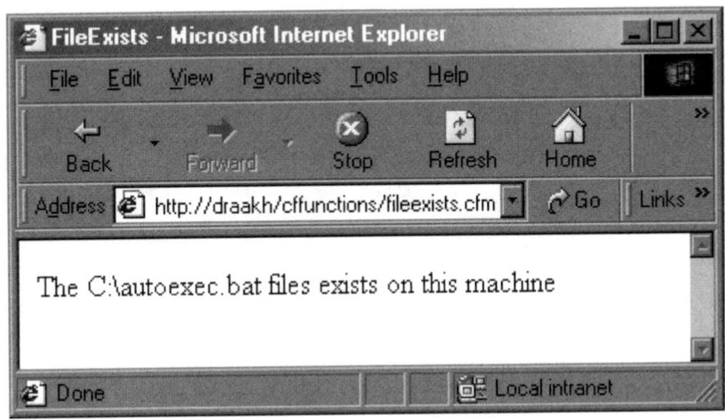

Figure 12.2 – FileExists checking for an autoexec.bat file.

If you type the path and filename directly into the function remember to surround it with speech marks. Try changing the contents of *TheFile* to check for files that do not exist.

Is that Dir there? DirectoryExists

A similar function to **FileExists** is **DirectoryExists**. This function checks to see if the given directory exists on the server.

The following template file demonstrates this function in use:

```
<HTML>
<HEAD>
	<TITLE>DirectoryExists</TITLE>
</HEAD>
<BODY>
	<CFSET TheDir="C:\Program Files">
	<CFIF DirectoryExists(TheDir)>
		<P>The <CFOUTPUT><B>#TheDir#</B></CFOUTPUT>
			directory exists on this machine
	<CFELSE>
		<P>This machine has no <CFOUTPUT><B>#TheDir#</B></CFOUTPUT>
directory
	</CFIF>
```

```
</BODY>
</HTML>
```

The author used this function for an application that collects electronic files from a user. The system has many users. To save work the ColdFusion server created directories for each user when required, when a file needed to be stored in the directory. This meant quite a complex checking procedure before each directory was created, part of which follows:

```
<CFIF DirectoryExists('#cookie.VaultRoot#archive/#form.moduleid#')>
<cfelse>
	<CFDIRECTORY action="CREATE" directory=
		"#cookie.VaultRoot#archive/#form.moduleid#">
</cfif>
```

Note the use of multiple variables to reference the path of the directory. This was partly because the code written needed to be portable across various ColdFusion servers, and the files may have needed to be stored in different drives on each different server. With this in mind, variables were created to store the paths to the files for each machine. This system went on to create further directories underneath this one to store individual user's work in each directory. As usual, all of this organizing goes on behind the scenes unknown to users.

Path processing: GetFileFromPath

Sometimes you will obtain the full filename and path of a file, but just need the file name. An example of this is when you use CFFILE to upload a file from a form. **GetFileFromPath** is a function that just returns the filename from the full file and path. The following template file demonstrates this in use:

```
<HTML>
<HEAD>
	<TITLE>Get From Path</TITLE>
</HEAD>
```

```
<BODY>
	<CFSET ThePath="C:\inetpub\wwwroot\index.cfm">
	<CFOUTPUT>
	<P>The path given was <b>#ThePath#</b><BR>
	The filename is <b>#GetFileFromPath(ThePath)#</b><BR>
	</CFOUTPUT>
</BODY>
</HTML>
```

Figure 12.3 shows **GetFileFromPath** working, along with the next function **GetDirectoryFromPath.**

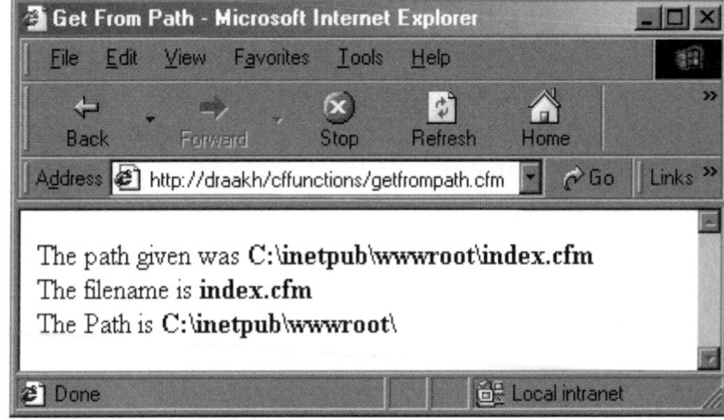

***Figure 12.3** – GetFileFromPath and GetDirectoryFromPath.*

More Paths: GetDirectoryFromPath

A function closely related to the previous is **GetDirectoryFromPath.** This function scans through the path and just returns the directory name. You can see the results of this function in figure 12.3 if you were to add the following line to the body of the above template:

```
The Path is <b>#GetDirectoryFromPath(ThePath)#</b><BR>
```

Both of these functions do not actually work with the file system of the server, but are merely text string manipulation functions which look for certain characters in the string. You do not need to use a path that exists on the server to use **GetFileFromPath** or **GetDirectoryFromPath.**

Paths again: ExpandPath

ExpandPath will generate a full path to a file if given the relative path. This is useful when you wish to find out, for instance where the template file that you are running is residing on the server. The following template is a modification of the CFDIRECTORY template we used in chapter 10:

```
<HTML>
<HEAD>
	<TITLE>Simple Directory by ExpandPath</TITLE>
</HEAD>
<BODY>
<CFDIRECTORY directory=#ExpandPath(".")#
	name="listdir">
<TABLE>
	<CFOUTPUT query="listdir">
		<TR>
			<TD>#Name# </td>
			<TD>#Size# </td>
			<TD>#Type# </td>
			<TD>#DateLastModified# </td>
			<TD>#Attributes#</td>
		</tr>
	</CFOUTPUT>
</table>
</BODY>
</HTML>
```

This template file, when placed in any directory will provide a listing of the contents of the directory. This could be useful if you wished to give users a list of files in directories on a server where directory browsing was not allowed. You would simply place this file in any directory you wanted them to browse. The path is expanded from a single full stop. Many people are familiar with the double full stop in DOS, which enables you to get to the parent directory. In the DOS world the single full stop means the current directory, which in ColdFusion terms is the directory in which the currently running template file is stored. Figure 12.4 shows the output of this file in relation to the *cffunction* directory on the author's ColdFusion server.

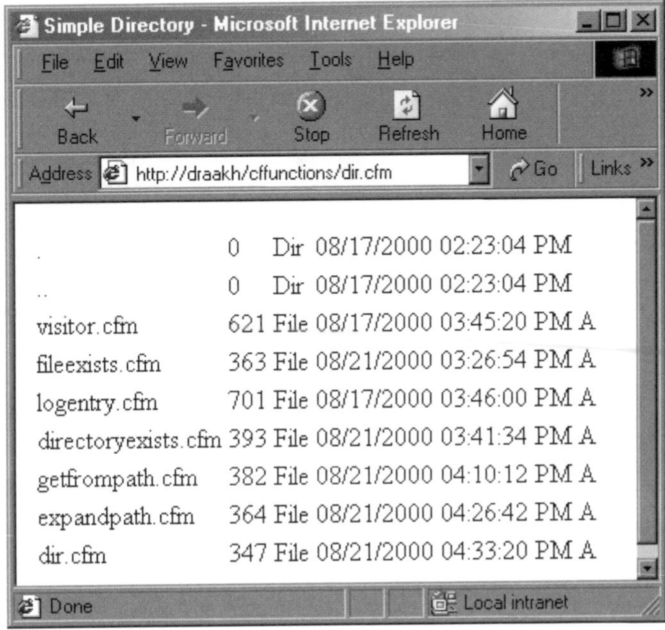

***Figure 12.4** – ExpandPath finding the current directory.*

Work it out with Evaluate

In chapter 11 we discussed local variables and while performing calculations had to use the **evaluate** function as follows:

```
#Evaluate(10000/100*tax)#
```

We used the **evaluate** function because if we wrote the calculation as *#(10000/100*tax)#* we get an error, and if we try it the other way *(10000/100*#tax#)*, we still don't have the calculation performed. Figure 12.5 shows the results for the two versions that work without an error. **Evaluate** forces the expression inside the brackets to be calculated, and allows variables to be processed without the hashes. We only need to hash the whole **evaluate** function, and not the variables inside.

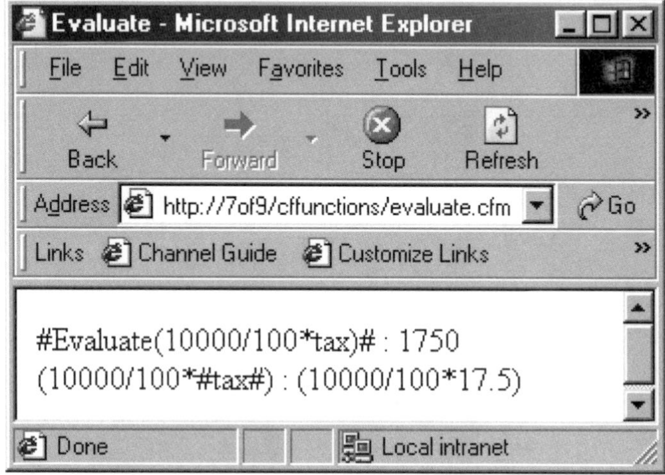

***Figure 12.5** – Calculation with evaluate and without.*

Think of a number: RandRange

Sometimes we want something to happen at random on our web pages. An example of this is Yahoo's random links. You click on a link on the Yahoo web site and it takes you to a random site from its vast database. ColdFusion makes this sort of behaviour possible by means of the **RandRange** function. **Randrange** is used in the following way:

```
RandRange(Firstnumber,SecondNumber)
```

Randrange will then pick a whole number between the first and second number. The following template file takes the results from the set of visitor book entries and picks a random one to display. Each time that you go to the web page a different name is displayed.

```
<HTML>
<HEAD>
      <TITLE>Random Quote</TITLE>
</HEAD>
<BODY>
<CFQUERY name="RandomQuote" datasource="MyLog">
      Select Name,Comment
      From VisitorBook
</CFQUERY>
<CFOUTPUT query="RandomQuote"
      maxrows="1"
      startrow="#RandRange(1,RandomQuote.Recordcount)#">
            "#Comment#" - #Name#
</CFOUTPUT>
</BODY>
</HTML>
```

Figure 12.6 shows one of the quotes returned by the **randrange** function. If you refresh the page then you should get another quote, unless ColdFusion decides to pick the same one.

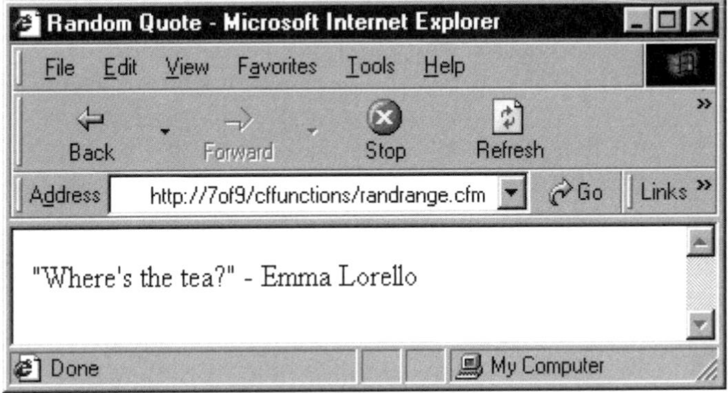

Figure 12.6 – A random quote generated by RandRange.

Rand

RandRange is actually just a more refined version of the **rand** function and returns a number in a specified range. The **rand** function picks a number between 0 and 1.

Make it more random: Randomize

As it is really quite difficult for a computer to pick true random numbers, the **randomize** function is provided to help give more random numbers. You get a number, and call randomize with it and it helps the random number generator to be even more random! You call the **randomize** function as follows:

```
<CFSET dummy=Randomize(42)>
```

The dummy variable is just a mechanism to trigger the **randomize** function and can be ignored. The 42 is the number that you seed the random number generator with. You would normally use the randomize function as above before using **rand** or **randrange**.

How long is that string: Len

Len is the first of a group of useful functions that allow the manipulation of strings. **Len**, given a string, will return its length. We can then use the length of the string in other string functions later. The following template uses CFHTTP to retrieve a web page and then measures the length of the page received. To maintain consistency we will use the *main.htm* page in the *cfdocs* page on your web server. If you wish to run this code make sure that you put your webserver name in the template file:

```
<HTML>
<HEAD>
```

```
    <TITLE>Len Function</TITLE>
</HEAD>
<BODY>
    <CFHTTP url="http://yourservername/cfdocs/main.htm">
    The Cfdocs index page is
    <CFOUTPUT>#Len(CFHTTP.FileContent)#</CFOUTPUT>
    Characters Long<BR>
</BODY>
</HTML>
```

In the above example **CFHTTP.FileContent** is a variable that contains the downloaded web page. It is a string so we can apply the **Len** function to it. Figure 12.7 shows the output of the above template.

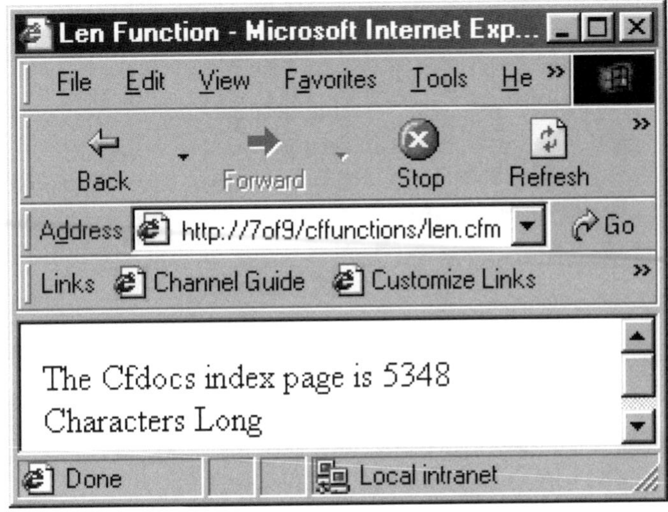

Figure 12.7 – The Len function at work.

String Manipulation Functions

To introduce the next few functions we will try to find some of the data that we cannot usually see out of the downloaded page and display it on the screen. The particular page that we are looking at contains some

Javascript, so we will create a template file that searches through a web page to find Javascript and then displays it.

String Searching: FindNoCase

FindNoCase searches through a string until it finds an occurrence of another string. When it has found this it returns the position of that string if it is there. If the search string is not in the main string then the function returns a zero. It takes the following format:

```
FindNoCase(SearchString, MainString, StartPosition)
```

- **MainString** is the string that you are searching through.
- **SearchString** is the string that you are looking for in the MainString.
- **StartPosition** is where the function starts to look through the MainString and is optional. This option is especially useful if you are looking for repeated occurrences of something in a string.

FindNoCase ignores the case of the text or string that you are looking for. If we are applying the function to our example we will use it to look for the start and end <SCRIPT> tags in our downloaded document to find the JavaScript. We need to change our template to read as follows:

```
<HTML>
<HEAD>
	<TITLE>FindNoCase</TITLE>
</HEAD>
<BODY>
	<CFHTTP url="http://7of9/cfdocs/main.htm">
	<CFOUTPUT>
		The Cfdocs index page is
		#Len(CFHTTP.FileContent)#
		Characters Long<BR>
		<CFSET StartJava=
```

```
                FindNoCase("SCRIPT",CFHTTP.FileContent)>
        <CFSET EndJava=
                FindNoCase("/SCRIPT",CFHTTP.FileContent)>
        Script tag begins at position #StartJava# and ends<BR>
        at position #EndJava#
    </CFOUTPUT>
</BODY>
</HTML>
```

Figure 12.8 shows the above template file running. We have stored the information gained from **FindNoCase** in two variables, *StartJava* and *EndJava,* and will use it later on. As we are using a web page that is of a standard format we have not included any error checking on the page. If we were writing this function for a working web site we would check to see if any of the functions had received a zero response and if so let the user know that there was no <SCRIPT> tag within the web page we are manipulating.

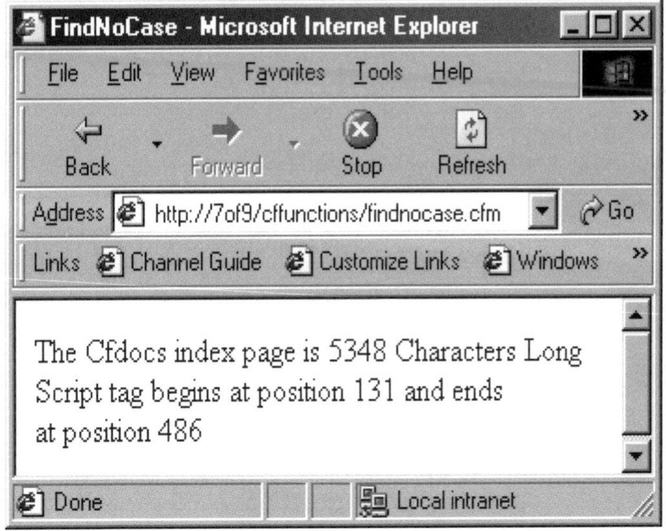

Figure 12.8 *– FindNoCase and Find in action.*

Find it in a String: Find

Find has exactly the same format as **FindNoCase** above. The only difference is that the case of the string that the function searches for is now important.

For example, if we were searching for *SCRIPT* and the string contained *script*, the function would probably not find a match and so return a zero.

To test **Find**, simply replace **FindNoCase** with **Find** in the above template file. The results should be the same as in figure 12.8 if you have used the correct case in your functions.

Cut that string apart: Mid

The **Mid** function returns part of a string that it is given based on a start position and character count. **Mid** takes the following format:

```
Mid(String, StartPosition, Characters)
```

- **String** is the string that you wish to process.
- **StartPosition** is the position in the string that you want the new string to begin.
- **Characters** is the number of characters from the StartPosition that you wish to include.

In our example we have the start and end of the Javascript that we wish to extract stored in variables so we can use this information to tell the **Mid** function which part of the string to extract. We can use the *StartJava* variable as it stands, as it contains the start position of the <SCRIPT> tag. However, the second number we require is the number of characters to include. We do not have this at the moment but we can derive this by taking the

StartJava variable away from the *EndJava* variable. Our nearly complete code will be as follows:

```
<HTML>
<HEAD>
    <TITLE>Mid</TITLE>
</HEAD>
<BODY>
    <CFHTTP url="http://7of9/cfdocs/main.htm">
    <CFOUTPUT>
        The Cfdocs index page is
        #Len(CFHTTP.FileContent)#
        Characters Long<BR>
        <CFSET StartJava=
            FindNoCase("SCRIPT",CFHTTP.FileContent)>
        <CFSET EndJava=
            FindNoCase("/SCRIPT",CFHTTP.FileContent)>
        Script tag begins at position #StartJava# and ends<BR>
        at position #EndJava#<BR>
        <CFSET JavaString=
            Mid(CFHTTP.FileContent,
                StartJava,EndJava-StartJava)>
        The actual script reads:<HR>
        #JavaString#
        <HR>
    </CFOUTPUT>
</BODY>
</HTML>
```

Figure 12.9 shows the above template in a web browser. You will notice that there are still a couple of errors in the script. These are the remnants of the <SCRIPT> tags that we chopped up to get our string. We could rewrite our **Mid** function code to exclude these parts of the code by adding and subtracting a few characters off our variables; however, we are going to introduce two more functions to do this on the new string we have just created.

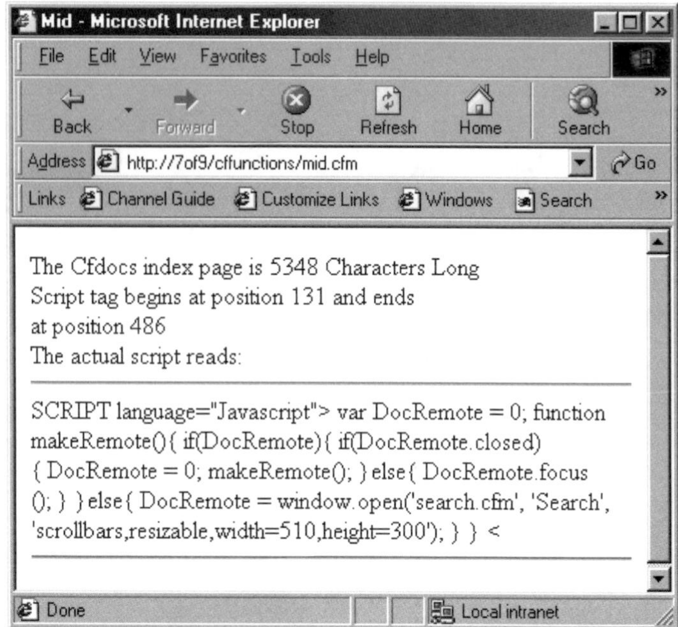

Figure 12.9 – The Mid function extracts our JavaScript.

Left a bit...

The **Left** function allows you to remove characters from the end of the given string. You give it the number and the string and it returns that number of characters from the start of the string. It has the following format:

```
Left(String,Characters)
```

- **String** is the string that we are working with and
- **Characters** are the amount of characters from the start that you want to receive back.

In our example, we need to remove the last character of our string, that is the symbol <. To remove this we can use the **Left** function to return all but one of the characters in the string. Again we do not have the number of characters but we can derive it by taking one away from the length of the string. We do this as follows:

```
<HTML>
<HEAD>
    <TITLE>Left</TITLE>
</HEAD>
<BODY>
    <CFHTTP url="http://7of9/cfdocs/main.htm">
    <CFOUTPUT>
        The Cfdocs index page is
        #Len(CFHTTP.FileContent)#
        Characters Long<BR>
        <CFSET StartJava=
            FindNoCase("SCRIPT",CFHTTP.FileContent)>
        <CFSET EndJava=
            FindNoCase("/SCRIPT",CFHTTP.FileContent)>
        Script tag begins at position #StartJava# and ends<BR>
        at position #EndJava#<BR>
        <CFSET JavaString=Mid(CFHTTP.FileContent,
            StartJava,EndJava-StartJava)>
        The actual script reads:<HR>
        #Left(JavaString,Len(JavaString)-1)#
        <HR>
    </CFOUTPUT>
</BODY>
</HTML>
```

This will remove the last character. We have nearly extracted all of the Javascript code.

Right a bit...

Right works the same way as **Left**, but returns the number of characters from the end of the string instead of the start. The format of **Right** is the same as of **Left**, that is:

```
Right(String,Characters)
```

- **String** is the string that we are working with and
- **Characters** are the amount of characters that you want returned.

We can use this in our example to cut off the start of the string. The end of the first <SCRIPT> tag is 30 characters into the string, so if we take 30 away from the length of the string we can derive the amount of characters that we wish to keep again. In the following template file we have moved the previous **Left** statement up into a variable again, so that it does not clutter the **Right** statement that we are looking at.

```
<HTML>
<HEAD>
    <TITLE>Right</TITLE>
</HEAD>
<BODY>
    <CFHTTP url="http://7of9/cfdocs/main.htm">
    <CFOUTPUT>
        The Cfdocs index page is
        #Len(CFHTTP.FileContent)#
        Characters Long<BR>
        <CFSET StartJava=
            FindNoCase("SCRIPT",CFHTTP.FileContent)>
        <CFSET EndJava=
            FindNoCase("/SCRIPT",CFHTTP.FileContent)>
        Script tag begins at position #StartJava# and ends<BR>
        at position #EndJava#<BR>
        <CFSET JavaString=Mid(CFHTTP.FileContent,
            StartJava,EndJava-StartJava)>
        <CFSET JavaString=Left(JavaString,Len(JavaString)-1)>
        The actual script reads:<HR>
        #Right(JavaString,Len(JavaString)-30)#
        <HR>
    </CFOUTPUT>
</BODY>
</HTML>
```

Figure 12.10 shows the above template file viewed in the browser.

If you are feeling adventurous you could now try to use the above functions to lay the Javascript out in a cleaner format. For instance, you could look for the semi-colon symbol ; and start printing the JavaScript after it on a new line.

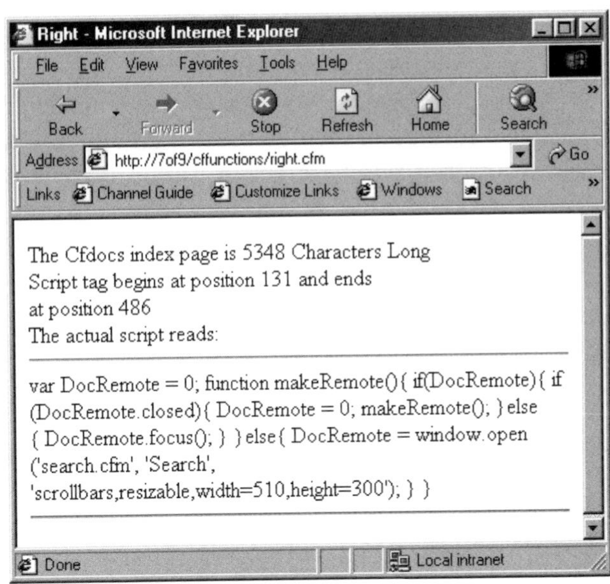

Figure 12.10 – The Right function finally extracts our Javascript.

Use of string manipulation like this can be very useful. Let us say that there was a web page, like a news headline page, that you looked at every day. If only you could put that on your web site. If you were to obtain permission to do this you could get ColdFusion to download the page to your web site. It could then use string manipulation to strip out all of the superfluous data (probably advertisements) and just get the useful text on to your pages.

You have to make sure that you put all of the error checking you can into a function like this. Bear in mind that if their web site goes down, its data will not be available for yours to use, so yours also may be less useful.

Convert the number with Val

Our final string function, **Val**, converts a number stored in a string to a value. It takes the following format:

```
Val(string)
```

where string contains a numeric value. If the string contains several only the first value is converted. This is useful as we sometimes wish to get values from a text field in a form, and then do some manipulation with them. The following template gets a numeric value as a text string from the user by means of a form, and then uses the value in our tax example.

```
<HTML>
<HEAD>
	<TITLE>Local Variables</TITLE>
</HEAD>
<BODY>
<CFIF IsDefined("Form.TaxString")>
	<CFSET tax=Val(Form.TaxString)>
	<CFOUTPUT>
		<BR>The basic rate of sales tax is #tax# %.
		<BR>Therefore everything that you buy has
		<BR>#tax# percent of its value added back onto it.
		<BR>So if you were to buy a car that cost &pound;10000
		<BR>You would have to pay an extra
		&pound;#Evaluate(10000/100*tax)# in tax
		<CFSET tax=tax*2>
		<BR>If the rate was doubled to #tax# %.
		<BR>Then you would pay an extra
		&pound;#Evaluate(10000/100*tax)# in tax!
	</CFOUTPUT>
<CFELSE>
	<FORM action="val.cfm" method="post">
		<P>Please type the tax rate in percent<BR>
		<Input type="text" name="TaxString">
		<Input type="Submit">
	</form>
</cfif>
</BODY>
</HTML>
```

In the above example the **Val** function may not always be needed, as ColdFusion is quite clever at matching the type of form fields into calculations. The **Val** function would, however, provide an extra level of checking in case the user typed some more text after the number, such as the percent sign.

Telling the time with Now

Second only to **IsDefined**, this is the function that I use the most. **Now** returns the current date and time as one object. You can instantly print the output of **Now** on to the web page or insert it straight into a *Date/Time* field in your database. **Now** requires no parameters, its format is as follows:

```
Now()
```

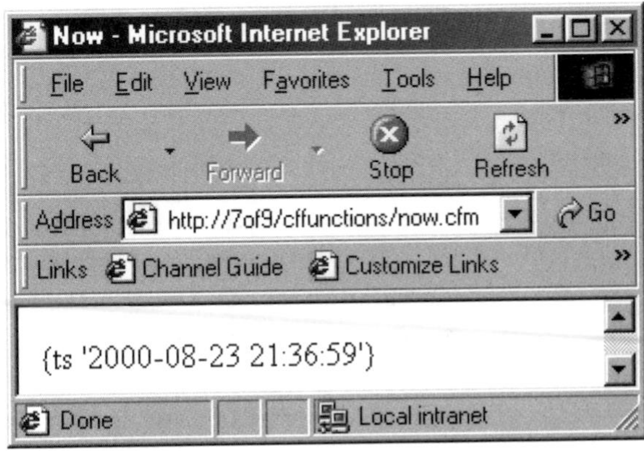

Figure 12.11 *– Basic output of Now.*

The following template simply prints the current date and time on the screen.

```
<HTML>
<HEAD>
	<TITLE>Now</TITLE>
</HEAD>
<BODY>
	<CFOUTPUT>
		#Now()#
	</CFOUTPUT>
</BODY>
</HTML>
```

Figure 12.11 shows the output of the above template. Notice how the date and time, although readable, are not formatted as clearly as they could be. If you had used the **Now** function to drop the current date and time into a database, when you read it back you would have had slightly more readable output. The following few functions used in conjunction with **Now** are used to improve the outputting of dates and times.

DateFormat

We start by using the **DateFormat** function to get a readable date from a *Date/Time* value. **DateFormat** has the following format:

```
DateFormat(Date,Format)
```

- *Date* is the date object that you want to manipulate and
- *Format* is how you want the date to look. If you omit this attribute you get a date in the format *Date-ThreeLetterMonth-TwoDigitYear*. If you add the format it needs to be a string consisting of character *d*'s for the date, *m*'s for the month and *y*'s for the years. Depending on how many characters you include the output changes. Table 12.1 shows some examples of this.

Table 12.1 – Formatting dates.

Format String	Example Date
"dd-mmm-yy" (Default)	23-Aug-00
"dddd, dd mmmm, yyyy"	Wednesday, 23 August, 2000
"dd/mm/yy"	23/08/00
"mm-dd-yyyy"	08-23-2000

TimeFormat

Time format extracts the time from a Date/Time object and formats it in a readable way. The format is similar to **DateFormat:**

```
TimeFormat(Time,Format)
```

- *Time* is the time object that you want to manipulate.
- *Format* is how you want the time to look. If you omit this attribute you get a time in the format *Hours:Minutes*. If you add the format it needs to be a string consisting of character *h*'s for the hours, *m*'s for the minutes and *s*'s for the seconds. Capital *H* signifies 24 hour clock, lowercase *h* is 12 hour clock. *t* is used to show am or pm. Depending on how many characters you include the output changes.

Table 12.2 shows some examples of this for five to six in the evening:

Table 12.2 – Formatting times.

Format String	Example Time
"hh:mm" (Default)	05:55
"HH:mm:ss"	17:55:34
"h-mm tt"	5-55 PM

CreateDateTime

Although **Now** is a very convenient way of creating a date and having a timestamp of the current time, we will at some stage need to create a Date and Time object for a future or past time. **CreateDateTime** can be used to do this. This function has the following format:

```
CreateDateTime(Year, Month, Day, Hour, Minutes, Seconds)
```

- **Year** is the year represented in 4 digits.
- **Month** is the month in digits.
- **Day** is the day of the month, not the day name.
- **Hour** is the hour in 24 hour clock format.
- **Minutes** is the minutes past the hour.
- **Seconds** are the amount of seconds elapsed in the minute.

To create a *Date/Time* object for exactly twenty past eight in the evening of the 4th October 1999 would require the following command:

```
<CFSET NewDate=CreateDateTime(1999,10,4,20,20,0)>
```

To get the user to actually enter a date is quite a task, the best way of doing this is via a set of drop down selectors as follows:

```
<HTML>
<HEAD>
	<TITLE>CreateDateTime</TITLE>
</HEAD>
<BODY>
<FORM>
	<SELECT NAME="Year">
		<CFLOOP INDEX="yr" FROM="1990" TO="2010" STEP="1">
		<OPTION><CFOUTPUT>#yr#</CFOUTPUT>
		</cfloop>
		<OPTION SELECTED>Year
	</SELECT>
	<SELECT NAME="Month">
		<OPTION value="1">January
		<OPTION value="2">February
		<OPTION value="3">March
		<OPTION value="4">April
		<OPTION value="5">May
		<OPTION SELECTED>Month
	</SELECT>
	<SELECT NAME="Day">
		<CFLOOP INDEX="day" FROM="1" TO="31" STEP="1">
			<OPTION><CFOUTPUT>#day#</CFOUTPUT>
		</cfloop>
		<OPTION SELECTED>Day
	</SELECT>
</form>
</BODY>
</HTML>
```

In the above example we have only coded five months, and just the year and the date, but with the code shown you could easily add the rest of the code to get all of the data from the user about the Date and Time object they wish to create. Note the way the month selection works. We display the month name, but the select tag passes the value through as its variable and not the name. This is a really good way of making your interface more user-friendly.

Figure 12.12 shows the above code when running. See if you can modify the template to add the extra selectors and pass the data acquired to another template that creates the object.

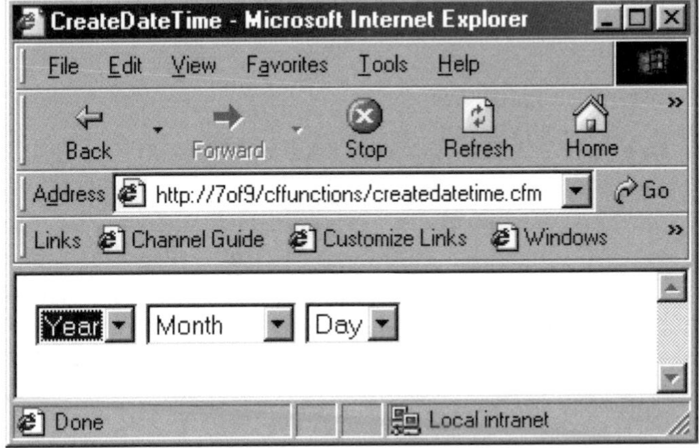

Figure 12.12 – Select boxes used to enter a date.

DayOfWeek

The final Date and Time functions of note are a method of getting the day of the week back from a date. The **DayOfWeek** function has the following format:

```
DayOfWeek(aDate)
```

- *aDate* is the date and time object corresponding to the day that you want to find.

The following template will show a number corresponding to what day it is today, with 1 representing Sunday and 7 representing Saturday:

```
<HTML>
<HEAD>
	<TITLE>DayOfWeek</TITLE>
</HEAD>
<BODY>
	<CFOUTPUT>
		#DayOfWeek(Now())#
	</CFOUTPUT>
</BODY>
</HTML>
```

DayOfWeekAsString

As the above template only shows a number, ColdFusion provides a method of converting that number back into a readable day. **DayOfWeekAsString** performs this for you in the following way:

```
DayOfWeekAsString(DayNumber)
```

- *DayNumber* is the number representing the day, with 1 representing Sunday through to 7 representing Saturday.

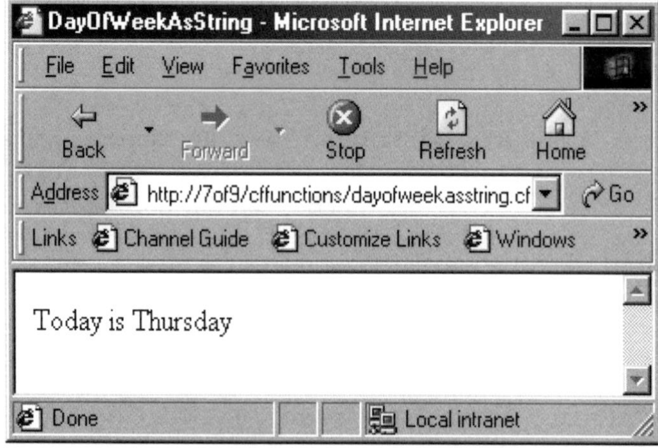

***Figure 12.13** – DayOfWeekAsString used to obtain the day.*

To return a readable version of what day it is we can use the following function call within a template which is shown in figure 12.13:

```
<HTML>
<HEAD>
	<TITLE>DayOfWeekAsString</TITLE>
</HEAD>
<BODY>
	<CFOUTPUT>
		Today is #DayOfWeekAsString(DayOfWeek(Now()))#
	</CFOUTPUT>
</BODY>
</HTML>
```

Chapter

13

Custom Tags

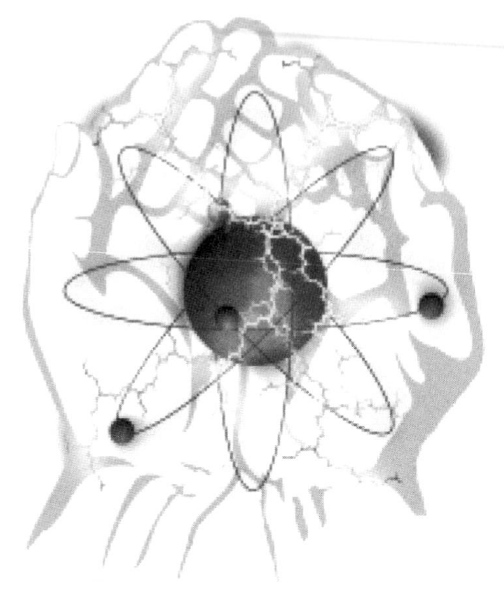

Introduction

Most programming languages have the ability to define procedures or functions. These are useful pieces of coding that the programmer writes and they are used repeatedly throughout their work. The programmer writes a procedure, gives it a name, and then whenever the procedure needs to be run calls it by name. This method hides complexity from the code, and saves re-writing out the code every time the programmer needs to use it. Functions as we have discussed in an earlier chapter, are a type of procedure. It would be useful to be able to write such procedures ourselves and not always have to code everything from scratch.

ColdFusion implements procedures in several different ways, all of which at first require a piece of code to be written and saved as a template file. We can collectively refer to all of these procedures that we write as custom tags.

Throughout this chapter we will use the following piece of code as a basis for our examples:

```
<CFQUERY name="addhit" datasource="MyLog">
Insert into Log (AccessDateAndTime,PageName,HostIPNum)
Values (#Now()#,'HomePage','#CGI.REMOTE_HOST#')
</CFQUERY>
```

You may remember this code from chapter 3. We use it to log an access to our web page. If we were designing a site we would want to log accesses to every page, but it would be tedious to have to put this code on each page manually. We can therefore turn this procedure into a custom tag. The first step is to save the above as a template file. Save it for the moment in a directory off your *wwwroot* called *custom*, and call the file *log.cfm*.

We can now discuss the various methods of calling this template file.

<CFINCLUDE>

<CFINCLUDE> places a ColdFusion template file into your current template file at the point you include the tag. Your template file executes just as if you had typed the included file in at that point. **<CFINCLUDE>** takes the following format:

```
<CFINCLUDE template="templatefilename">
```

You can include the full server path to the template file, or just the template filename if it is in the same directory as the calling template. You can also include the relative path to it, so that if there are some template files in a directory off the current directory, you can include them if you want as well.

We can demonstrate this by modifying our existing *index.cfm* on our main web page. We need to alter it so it contains the <CFINCLUDE> as follows:

```
<HTML>
<TITLE>My Web Page</TITLE>
<BODY>
<CFQUERY datasource="MyLog" name="Hits">
	Select	*
	from Log
</CFQUERY>
<CENTER>
<H1>My Web Page</H1>
<P>Welcome to my page, glad you could come!
<P>Here is what I look like: <BR><BR>
<IMG src="mugshot.jpg">
<P>You are the
<CFOUTPUT>
#Hits.Recordcount#
</CFOUTPUT>
 visitor to this site.</P>
</CENTER>
<CFINCLUDE template="custom/log.cfm">
</BODY>
</HTML>
```

Save the above code as *index.cfm* in the root of your web server. If you view this page through a browser it should not look any different to our original example in chapter 3. The point is that the code is executed no differently; however, it should now be easier to debug and easier to program. Any of the pages that we want to log access to can now be logged by placing the code:

```
<CFINCLUDE template="custom/log.cfm">
```

somewhere in the template file.

You may have noticed, though, that if we move the calling template file into a sub directory, the above tag will not work, as the relative path to *log.cfm* will have changed. You may also have noticed that no matter what the name of the page that calls the *log.cfm*, the tag always stores the page name *HomePage* in the database. A useful facility would be to pass a parameter to the custom tag that contained the current page that needed to be logged.

Custom Tags

While using the <CFINCLUDE> tag to include template files is useful, it cannot be used to pass parameters to the called file and you have to be careful about from where you call the file. Figure 13.1 shows the *CustomTags* directory on a ColdFusion web server. Every template file placed in this directory becomes a custom tag for use by all of the template files on the server, no matter where they are stored.

To call a template file from the CustomTags directory you use the following format:

```
<CF_templateName attribute=value ...>
```

- *templateName* is the name of the file in the CustomTags directory, without the *.cfm* extension. You can also use the name of a file in the current directory as well, if you do not want to place your template file in the CustomTags directory.

Remember, if you are using files outside of the CustomTags directory it needs to be copied into each of the directories where calling templates are stored.

- *attribute* is the name of the parameter that you wish to pass to the template file.
- *value* is the value of the specific attribute.

You may pass as many attributes as required in this way.

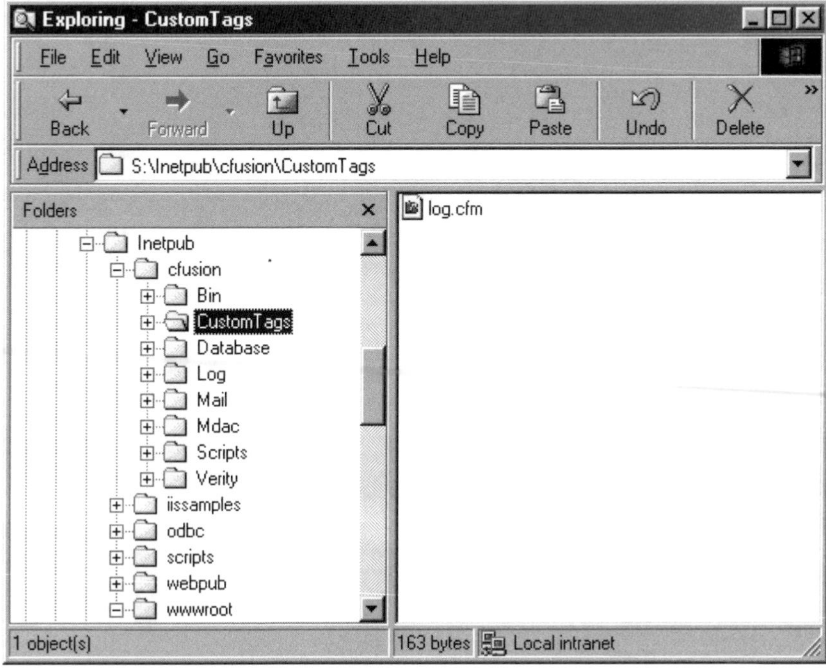

***Figure 13.1** – The CustomTags directory on the web server.*

Next we need to modify our existing *index.cfm* file to call the custom tag instead of using <CFINCLUDE>. Change your *index.cfm* so that it now reads as follows:

```
<HTML>
<TITLE>My Web Page</TITLE>
<BODY>
<CFQUERY datasource="MyLog" name="Hits">
      Select      *
      from  Log
```

```
</CFQUERY>
<CENTER>
<H1>My Web Page</H1>
<P>Welcome to my page, glad you could come!
<P>Here is what I look like: <BR><BR>
<IMG src="mugshot.jpg">
<P>You are the
<CFOUTPUT>
#Hits.Recordcount#
</CFOUTPUT>
 visitor to this site.</P>
</CENTER>
<CF_LOG>
</BODY>
</HTML>
```

The above code does not look very different from previous code but now we can log a site hit to any page on the whole site simply by the addition of the command:

```
<CF_LOG>
```

in the template file as shown above.

Custom Tag Attributes

This log file is still storing the same page name whichever template calls it, so we need to modify the call by adding an attribute to it, as follows:

```
<CF_LOG pageName="HomePage">
```

This now passes the attribute *pageName* into the custom tag with the value *HomePage*. At the moment, though, the tag does not use the attribute, so we need to modify the tag code to accept the attribute and store it. Load in your *log.cfm* from your CustomTags directory and edit it so it reads as follows:

```
<CFQUERY name="addhit" datasource="MyLog">
      Insert into Log (AccessDateAndTime,PageName,HostIPNum)
      Values (#Now()#,'#attributes.pageName#','#CGI.REMOTE_HOST#')
</CFQUERY>
```

Notice how we refer to the attributes that have been passed to the custom tag. They work in the same way as other variables in that they are referred to in the custom tag as:

```
Attributes.AttributeName
```

Once they have been passed to the tag they can be used in the same way as other types of variables. The attribute variable is only available inside the custom tag, so as soon as the custom tag processing ends the variable is discarded.

There is one further problem with our tag. Now that we have added the functionality to send the page name to the tag, figure 13.2 shows what happens if we forget to pass the page name.

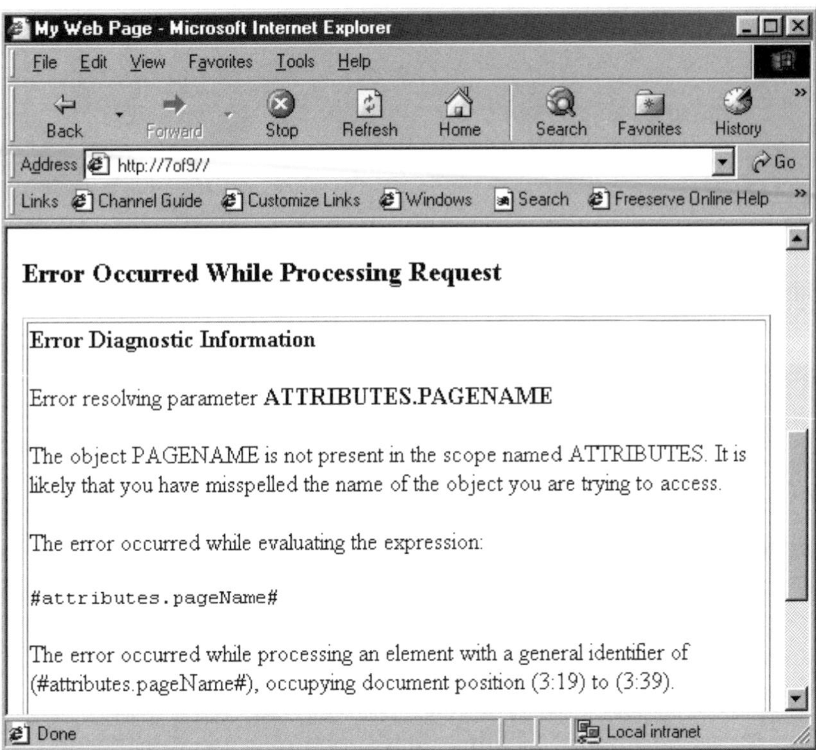

***Figure 13.2** – Forgetting the attribute in a custom tag.*

To prevent the error shown in Figure 13.2, we need to change the custom tag so that it checks for the existence of the attribute, and if it does not exist replaces it with some different data as follows:

```
<CFIF isDefined("attributes.pageName")>
	<CFSET page="#attributes.pageName#">
<CFELSE>
	<CFSET page="#CGI.script_name#">
</cfif>
<CFQUERY name="addhit" datasource="MyLog">
	Insert into Log (AccessDateAndTime,PageName,HostIPNum)
	Values (#Now()#,'#page#','#CGI.REMOTE_HOST#')
</CFQUERY>
```

This template first checks to see if the attribute exists. If it does it stores its contents in a temporary variable called page. If not it stores the CGI variable that contains the name of the script that the server is running in the page variable. Once this is over the query stores the page variable in the database, which prevents an error. You can now call the log tag from anywhere with or without a page name and it will work correctly.

Once you are happy with your custom tag's function you will find that you begin to create tags all of the time. The beauty of them is that you can reuse the code within these tags across various different web sites or pages. For instance, the author has used slightly different variations of the *log.cfm* over many different applications. Using custom tags allows you to develop new applications quicker by reusing your code.

Remember that if you are developing code on a shared ColdFusion system you have to be careful with your custom tags. If you place your tag into the CustomTags directory it will be available to all of the ColdFusion scripts on the system, that is everyone's, not just yours. With this in mind it is sometimes better to store your custom tags locally, that is, in the directory where you will be calling them. If you are creating a secure application on a shared server it is recommended that you store these tags locally.

Now that you are comfortable with custom tags try and put the code that reports the page hits back on the web site into a custom tag. You may even be able to add an attribute that only returns the hits that have been logged for that page!

Returning Values

We have seen how we can send values to custom tags but what about sending values back? There is a special variable type that is used within a custom tag called the caller variable. If you set a caller variable within a custom tag this becomes a local variable in the calling template. You set caller variables using the following format:

```
<CFSET caller.variableName=value>
```

You can refer to the variable using just its name within the custom tag and it becomes a local variable in the template that invoked the tag on return. We could modify our *log.cfm* so that it returned the hit count on that current page automatically using this method. We therefore need to add the following to the end of our *log.cfm* custom tag:

```
<CFQUERY name="hitcount" datasource="MyLog">
	Select * from Log
	where PageName = '#page#'
</CFQUERY>
<CFSET caller.hitcount=hitcount.Recordcount>
```

You do not have to modify any of the files that call the tag after this change unless you want to use the variable that is returned. We could modify the *index.cfm* file to only show hits to the main page by invoking the <CF_LOG> tag before we output the record count and then use the *hitcount* variable instead.

<CFEXIT>

This tag is used to stop the processing of a custom tag. It can, however, be called with several different methods that lead to different behaviour depending on where the tag is when it is executed. <CFEXIT> takes the following format:

```
<CFEXIT method="Method">
```

Method determines the effect that you want the custom tag to have and can be omitted. If included it has the following options:

- **ExitTag.** This stops the current custom tag in its tracks and returns execution to the template file that had called it. This is the default method for the tag.
- **ExitTemplate.** This stops not only the current custom tag but stops the template file that called it.
- **Loop.** This option stops the custom tag where it appears but then gets the custom tag to re-run.

If the <CFEXIT> is called when it is in a normal template file, not in a custom tag, it purely stops the template that is being run. Any processing that has been done to that point still stands, so the user would still see a web page if one had been created before the <CFEXIT>.

Application.cfm

The *application.cfm* is a special custom tag that if placed in a directory, will automatically be included into any template file that is executed in that directory or any below it. The *application.cfm* file is just a standard template file that is engineered to run before anything else.

The application template file is useful because if placed in a directory structure it can apply certain commands to all templates.

For example, figure 13.3 shows a directory structure on the ColdFusion server.

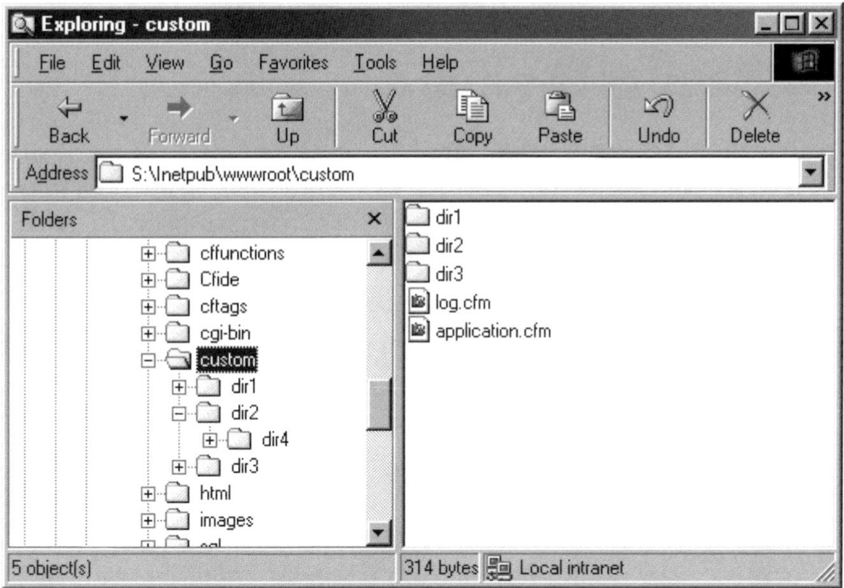

Figure 13.3 – Application.cfm applies to all child directories.

When the *application.cfm* is placed in the custom directory, its code will be run when any tag in custom, dir1, dir2, dir3 and dir4 is executed. It will not, however, effect any tags in the HTML or image directories shown.

If we were to put the contents of our logging tag, *log.cfm* into our *application.cfm* it would automatically log every access to every page on our web server. If we were to put a user authentication routine in the *application.cfm*, it would ensure that no template file within the protected directories could be loaded by any unauthorized user.

ColdFusion uses the first *application.cfm* that it comes across. This means that one *application.cfm* could override another one. For instance in figure 13.3, if we were to place a different *application.cfm* in dir4, everything in this directory and below (if there were more directories in dir4) would be influenced by that new application template.

OnRequestEnd.cfm

OnRequestEnd.cfm is a special template file that works in exactly the same way as *application.cfm*, apart from that it is always run at the end of the called template file. This is used in conjunction with the *application.cfm* file to, for example, close off any tags that have been opened in the *application.cfm* file or to provide consistent footer information over a series of web pages.

<CFAPPLICATION>

<CFAPPLICATION> is a special tag that is used within an *application.cfm* template. It takes the following format:

```
<CFAPPLICATION name="ApplicationName"
clientmanagement="YesNo"
clientstorage="Type"
sessiontimeout=TimeSpan
applicationtimeout=TimeSpan>
```

The attributes of the <CFAPPLICATION> tag set various parameters for your application:

- **Name** is the name of your application.
- **Clientmanagement** instructs the application to use client variables, normally this is set to *No*, so if you want to use them set it to *Yes.*
- **Clientstorage.** This defines where you want to store the client variables. The types are:
  - **Datasource.** The variables are stored in the data source defined in the ColdFusion Administrator Variables page.
  - **Registry.** This stores the variables in the server Registry.
  - **Cookie.** This stores the variables on the client, in a cookie file.
- **Sessionmanagement.** Lets the application know that you will be using session variables.

- **Sessiontimeout** and **applicationtimeout** define the timeout on the session or application variables that the application has defined. You create the timespan using the **CreateTimespan** function which takes the following format:

```
CreateTimeSpan(days,hours,minutes,seconds)
```

Use of the <CFAPPLICATION> tag is not mandatory in an *application.cfm* file. If you omit the tag your application template will still be added to all of the templates under its influence.

Once you have enabled the various variables in your *application.cfm* file you can define them and use them within your application.

Chapter

14

Using Cookies to Track Users

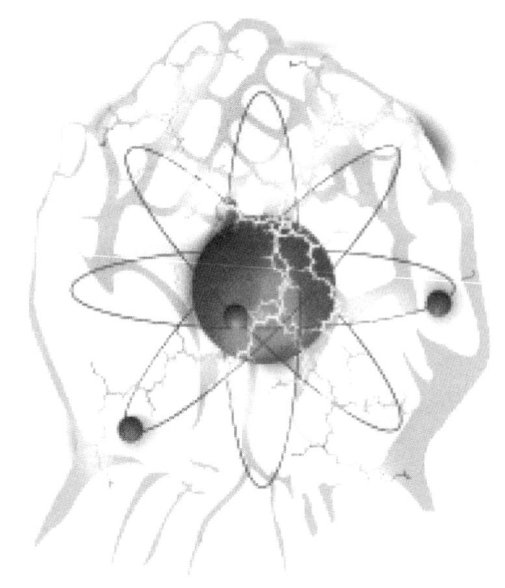

Introduction

This and the following two chapters will explore three common functions of a web site and discuss how to code them. In this chapter we discuss the use of cookies to track returning visitors to our web pages.

We use the IP number to track a user when they are looking at our site. While the user is visiting it is assumed that they will be using the same IP number. We can see how the particular user moved through our site. If, however, they are using a dial-up connection to the Internet the next time that they visit our site they will very probably have a different IP number. To get around this we can store a cookie on their machine, which we will look for on their return. Although not foolproof, this may give us a more accurate indication of who is coming back to our site on subsequent occasions.

In chapter 7 we discussed a way of establishing whether a user had returned to our site on several occasions. We suggested the following process for tracking our returning users:

- Add an extra column, called cookies, to your log database.
- Create a new table called cookies with an ID field that uses AutoNumber.
- In your accesslog code, check to see if the user has a cookie for your site.
  - If so, find the cookie value and write it to your access log.
  - If not, insert a new record into your cookies table. Retrieve this record to get its unique ID (from its AutoNumber field). Set a new cookie on the client machine using this number.

We will now describe how to perform the above steps.

The first step, which is performed once only, requires a modification to our Log table. Load Microsoft Access and open up your *Accesslog* database which will result in the screen shown in figure 14.1.

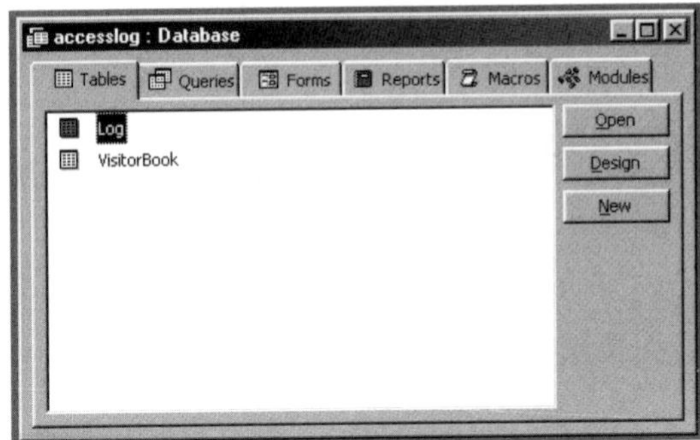

***Figure 14.1** – The accesslog table revisited.*

Select the log table and click on design. Figure 14.2 shows the screen that follows which is the design screen of our log table.

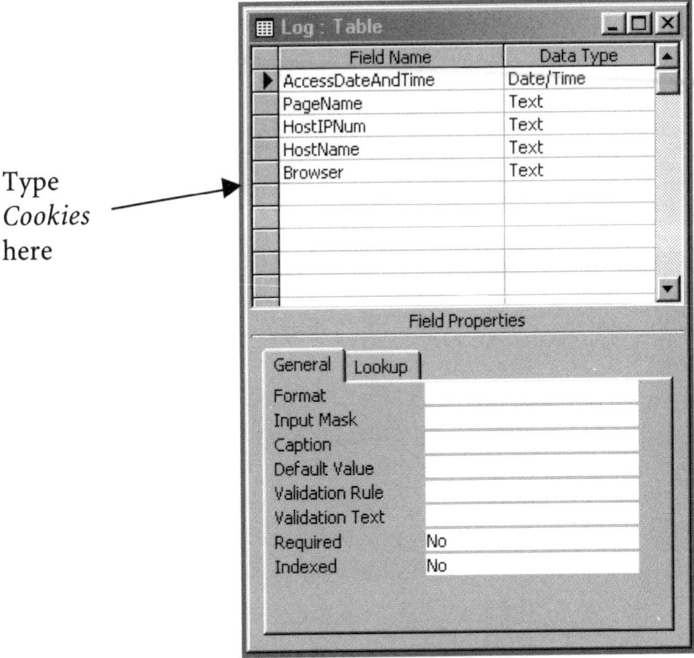

***Figure 14.2** – The design view of log.*

Click on the empty box in the *Field Name* column just under the field called *Browser.* Type the word *Cookies* into this box. In the data type box to the right of *Cookies*, select the option *Number* from the pull down box as shown in figure 14.3.

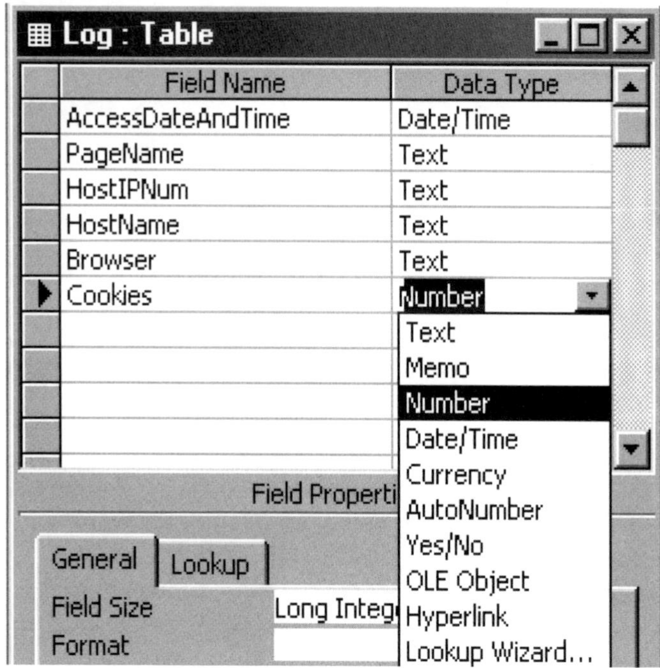

***Figure 14.3** – Adding the Number column to our Log table.*

Close the Log table and we can now create our new table that will store the cookies and cookie numbers. We need to set this up once and never repeat the process. You should now be back at the screen shown in figure 14.1. This time click on the new button and select design view and click on OK. You will see a blank table, which you need to set up as shown in figure 14.4.

Once you have set up this table, and saved it as cookies, the rest of the changes need to be done within your *log.cfm* custom tag.

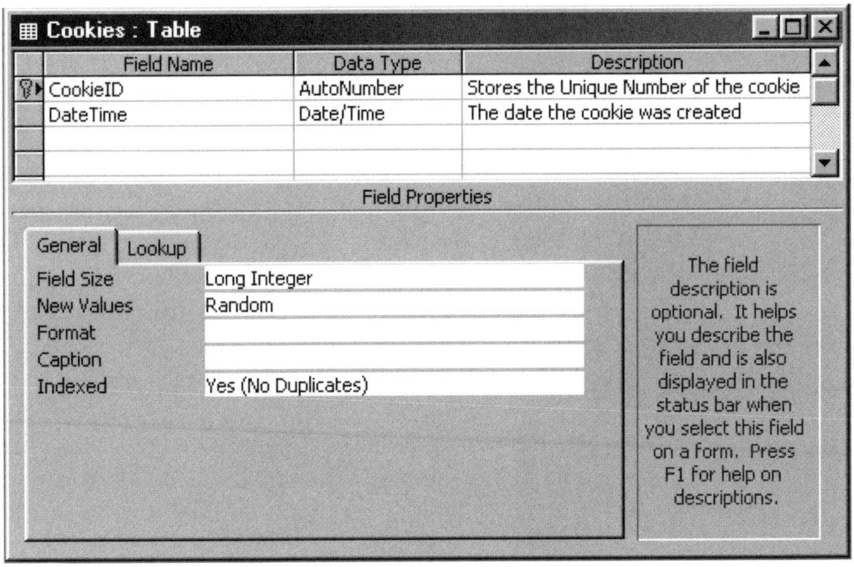

Cookies : Table

Field Name	Data Type	Description
CookieID	AutoNumber	Stores the Unique Number of the cookie
DateTime	Date/Time	The date the cookie was created

Field Properties

General | Lookup

Field Size	Long Integer
New Values	Random
Format	
Caption	
Indexed	Yes (No Duplicates)

The field description is optional. It helps you describe the field and is also displayed in the status bar when you select this field on a form. Press F1 for help on descriptions.

***Figure 14.4** – Our new cookie table.*

Currently, this tag checks to see if the *pageName* attribute is defined, and sets the local variable *page* to the same value. If the *pageName* variable is not defined, the tag sets the *page* variable to the name of the running template file by means of the *CGI.script_name* CGI variable. Once it has defined the variable, we then can store the data in the database. Up to now the *log.cfm* file looks as follows:

```
<CFIF isDefined("attributes.pageName")>
      <CFSET page="#attributes.pageName#">
<CFELSE>
      <CFSET page="#CGI.script_name#">
</cfif>
<CFQUERY name="addhit" datasource="MyLog">
      Insert into Log (AccessDateAndTime,PageName,HostIPNum)
      Values (#Now()#,'#page#','#CGI.REMOTE_HOST#')
</CFQUERY>
```

We need to ascertain the value of the cookie, creating a new one if necessary, and store it in a temporary variable that we then can add to the log database. We look for the cookie in the same way as the attributes variable by using:

```
<CFIF isDefined("cookie.userid")>
```

If it is defined we just pop it into a temporary variable, using:

```
<CFSET userid=#cookie.userid#>
```

If the cookie is not defined, and therefore has not been set, it is more complicated. First we need to store the current time so that we can retrieve the cookie we have just created by means of this time. We do this by use of a variable and query as follows:

```
<CFSET TimeNow=Now()>
```

We then have to create a new cookie value by inserting this variable just created into the cookie field as follows:

```
<CFQUERY name="createcookie" datasource="MyLog">
	Insert into Cookies (DateTime)
	Values (#TimeNow#)
</CFQUERY>
```

We now need to get the cookie we have just created back quickly. So we immediately run another query to retrieve it:

```
<CFQUERY name="getcookie" datasource="MyLog">
	select CookieID
from Cookies
	where DateTime = #TimeNow#
</CFQUERY>
```

We have now successfully created and retrieved a new cookie ID. All that remains is to store it in a variable temporarily:

```
<CFSET UserID=getcookie.CookieID>
```

and setting the new cookie on the client with the <CFCOOKIE> tag:

```
<CFCOOKIE Name="UserID" value=getcookie.CookieID expires="never">
```

Finally we modify our log insert by adding the extra variable:

```
<CFQUERY name="addhit" datasource="MyLog">
      Insert into Log (AccessDateAndTime,PageName,HostIPNum,Cookies)
      Values (#Now()#,'#page#','#CGI.REMOTE_HOST#','#UserID#')
</CFQUERY>
```

A complete listing of our modified *log.cfm* file is shown below:

```
<CFIF isDefined("cookie.userid")>
<CFSET userid=#cookie.userid#>
<CFELSE>
<CFSET TimeNow=Now()>
<CFQUERY name="createcookie" datasource="MyLog">
      Insert into Cookies (DateTime)
      Values (#TimeNow#)
</CFQUERY>
<CFQUERY name="getcookie" datasource="MyLog">
      select CookieID
from Cookies
      where DateTime = #TimeNow#
</CFQUERY>
<CFSET UserID=getcookie.CookieID>
<CFCOOKIE Name="UserID" value=getcookie.CookieID expires="never">
</CFIF>
<CFIF isDefined("attributes.pageName")>
      <CFSET page="#attributes.pageName#">
<CFELSE>
      <CFSET page="#CGI.script_name#">
</cfif>
<CFQUERY name="addhit" datasource="MyLog">
      Insert into Log (AccessDateAndTime,PageName,HostIPNum,Cookies)
      Values (#Now()#,'#page#','#CGI.REMOTE_HOST#','#UserID#')
</CFQUERY>
```

Once this is stored in your custom tag directory you will be able to use the cookies to see who has revisited your site. If you get visits with different dates and the same cookie value congratulations! Your site has brought people back! To get meaningful data back you will probably need to make a few changes to your tracking templates that list your site hits.

Chapter 15

Securing Web Pages

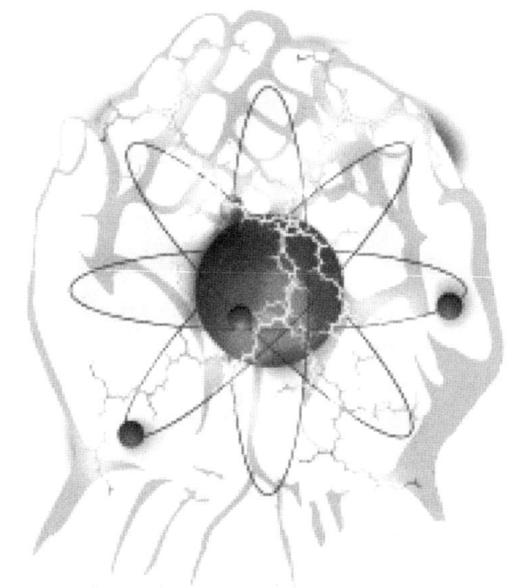

Introduction

This chapter demonstrates the use of the *application.cfm* file to provide a level of security within a directory of our web site. We will deny access to this directory without a valid username and password. All of the template files within this area will then be protected.

User authentication

As the data available from your site logs could be classed as secure, we will move It into a separate directory and add password protection via the application tag. If you have been following all of the examples in this book you should have a template file in your book directory called *logs.cfm*. Create a new directory off your *wwwroot* and call it *secure*. Move your *logs.cfm* template into that directory. If you are not sure of the state of your *logs.cfm* file it should read as follows:

```
<HTML>
<TITLE>My web page access log</TITLE>
<CFQUERY datasource="MyLog" name="HitList">
      Select HostIPNum,AccessDateAndTime
      from Log
</CFQUERY>
<BODY>
<P>This page lists the accesses to my pages. (Apart from this one)
<P>
<TABLE border =1>
<TR><TD>Access Time</TD> <TD>Host IP Number</TD></TR>
<CFOUTPUT query="HitList" maxrows=10>
<TR>
      <TD>#AccessDateandTime#</TD>
      <TD>#HostIPNum#</TD>
</TR>
</CFOUTPUT>
</TABLE>
```

```
Total Hits : <CFOUTPUT>#HitList.Recordcount#</CFOUTPUT>
</BODY>
</HTML>
```

Point your browser at this file in its new secure directory and it will look like figure 15.1.

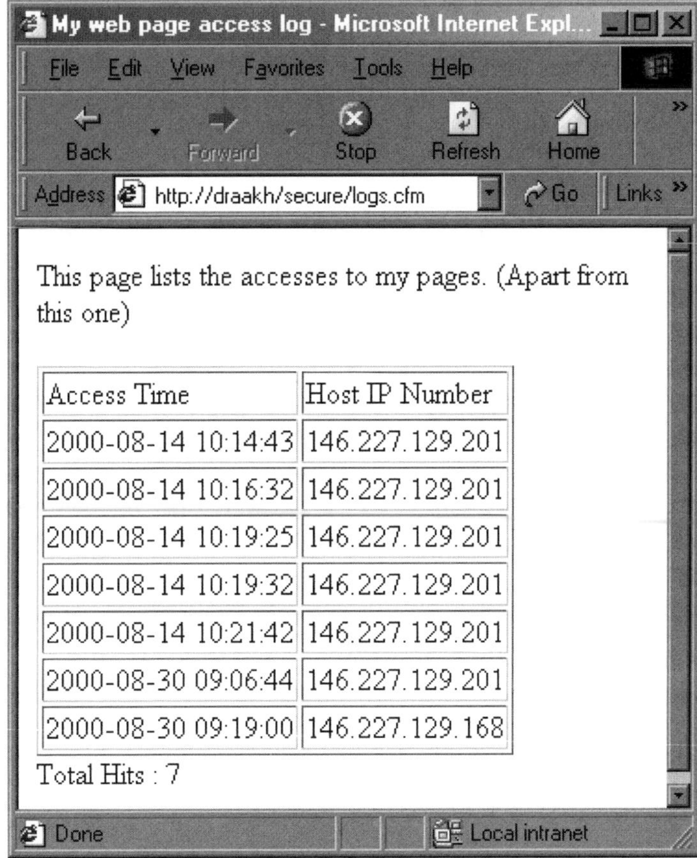

***Figure 15.1** – The tracking template in a new directory.*

The next task is to create a form that will be used to log the user in. The following form asks the user for a username and password as shown in figure 15.2:

```
<FORM action="check.cfm" method="POST">
      <TABLE>
            <TR><TD>Name</td>
```

```
			<TD><INPUT type="text"
					name="uname"></td>
		</tr>
		<TR><TD>Password</td>
			<TD><INPUT type="password" name="password"></td>
		</tr>
		<TR><TD></td>
			<TD align="right">
<INPUT type="Submit" Value="Login"></td>
		</tr>
	</table>
</form>
```

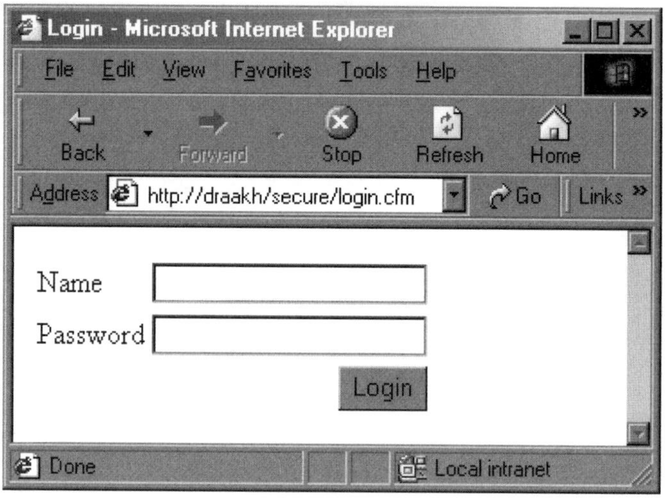

***Figure 15.2** – The login form for the secure area.*

When the user clicks on the Login button in figure 15.2 they will be taken to a page that checks that their username and password match those on file or stored in the template. If they match, we will set a cookie on a temporary basis that says that they are logged in. If we do not set an expiry date on this cookie, it will allow them to move about freely through the secure area until they turn off their browser or log off. As their cookie is never written to the user's disk it provides a higher level of security for the site.

Our *application.cfm* therefore needs to check for the authentication cookie, and if it does not exist prompt the user for the username and password via the form in figure 15.2. Save the following template as *application.cfm* in your secure directory:

```
<CFIF NOT ISDEFINED("COOKIE.AUTHENTICATEDUSER") AND
GetFileFromPath(CGI.script_name) NEQ "check.cfm">
	<FORM action="check.cfm" method="POST">
		<INPUT type="hidden" name="script" value="
			<CFOUTPUT>
				#GetFileFromPath(CGI.script_name)#
			</CFOUTPUT>">
		<TABLE>
			<TR><TD>Name</td>
				<TD><INPUT type="text" name="uname"></td>
			</tr>
			<TR><TD>Password</td>
				<TD><INPUT type="password"
				 name="password"></td>
			</tr>
			<TR><TD></td>
				<TD align="right">
				<INPUT type="Submit" Value="Login"></td>
			</tr>
		</table>
	</form>
	<CFABORT>
<CFELSE>
</cfif>
<CFIF ISDEFINED("COOKIE.AUTHENTICATEDUSER") AND
GetFileFromPath(CGI.script_name) NEQ "check.cfm">
	<a href="logout.cfm">Log Out</A>
</CFIF>
```

The above application template:

- First checks to see if the authenticated cookie exists.
  - It then checks to see whether the *check.cfm* template is running, as then it does not need to execute further.
  - If the cookie does not exist it displays our login form. When this form is displayed the tag aborts to stop the protected page appearing.

- If the user is authenticated all the tag does is provide a link to *logout.cfm*, which simply expires the cookie as follows:

```
<HTML>
<HEAD>
	<TITLE>Logout</TITLE>
</HEAD>
<BODY>
	<CFCOOKIE name="AUTHENTICATEDUSER"
		value="NO" expires="Now">
	<P>Bye!<BR>
	You are logged out of the secure area.
</BODY>
</HTML>
```

When the user submits the form, it passes its data to the file *check.cfm*. As the *check.cfm* file is in the secure directory, it will have the application template applied to it first, which is why we checked for it in the application file. If we were to have omitted this check we would have ended up with two forms for the user to interact with, which would be confusing. Save the following template as *check.cfm* in your secure directory:

```
<HTML>
<HEAD></HEAD>
<BODY>
	<CFIF form.uname eq "auser" AND form.password eq "jamesbond">
		<CFCOOKIE name="AUTHENTICATEDUSER" value="YES">
		<a href="logout.cfm">Log Out</A>
		<CFINCLUDE template="#form.script#">
	<CFELSE>
		<P><font color="#FF0000">Sorry</font> that username or
						password is incorrect.
		<P>Please try again.
		<FORM action="check.cfm" method="POST">
		<INPUT type="hidden" name="script"
				value="<CFOUTPUT>#form.script#</CFOUTPUT>">
			<TABLE>
				<TR><TD>Name</td>
					<TD><INPUT type="text" name="uname"></td>
				</tr>
```

```
                <TR><TD>Password</td>
                    <TD><INPUT type="password"
                                name="password"></td>
                </tr>
                <TR><TD></td>
                    <TD align="right"><INPUT type="Submit"
                                     Value="Login"></td>
                </tr>
            </table>
        </form>
    </cfif>
</BODY>
</HTML>
```

The above template has the username and password hard coded in, but you could easily pull the data from a table with usernames and passwords in them, if you wanted to deal with multiple users. If the user's credentials match those on file, the authenticated cookie is set. The cookie's value is irrelevant here, as its existence signifies the user has passed the check. It then provides a link to the logout URL, as the application ignores this template and then includes the original template that was requested before the application template kicked in, which it gets from a hidden field passed to it via the form.

If the user fails the credential check then the login form is displayed again with a message that prompts the user to try again. Figure 15.3 shows the output of a failed login attempt. The hidden field for the script name is passed through again, because if we used the same logic as in the previous form we would then send *check.cfm* through, and not the original script name.

Remember that while this provides some security, this is not a totally secure site. If, for example, your secure directory was handling credit card information you would need additional security, as data sent at the moment is not sent securely.

***Figure 15.3** – A failed login gives the user another attempt.*

Also be aware that we have put no real navigational links in this application. For example, if you click on the logout link it would be good to give the user an opportunity to get back into the non-secure site, as at the moment we just leave them at the end of a thread with nowhere to go. A good way of ensuring your navigational structures is to embed a navigation bar in all of the templates by using the *application.cfm* template.

Try adding some other template files to the directory now. Add a standard *.htm* file and a graphics file as well into the secure directory. See if you can work out if the password protection will work on these files and explain the results.

Chapter 16

Scheduling Tasks

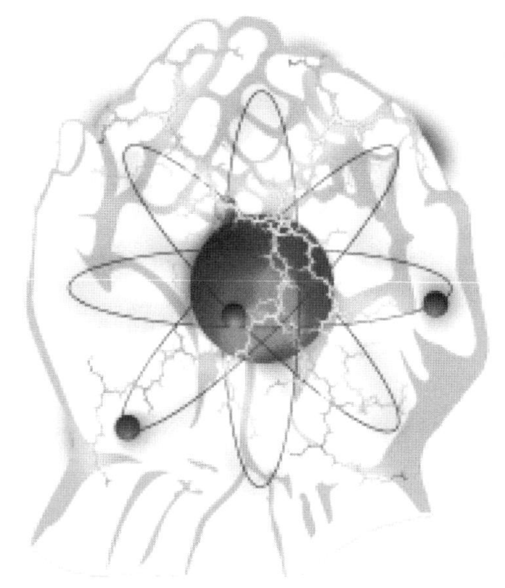

Introduction

In this chapter we will look at how we use the scheduling features of ColdFusion.

Scheduling is provided to perform certain events at certain times. You could use scheduling to do many things, for example:

- To check a POP3 server periodically for email to download.
- To check a diary database and alert the user if any events are imminent.
- To run a task that checks to see if a server is online and warn if it does not.
- To perform a regularly occurring query and store the data, so that users can get straight to the data without waiting for the query to run.

This chapter describes a function similar to the latter example. We schedule a task that counts the number of accesses to our web site and emails us with the results at a predefined interval.

Scheduling tasks

ColdFusion gives the developer the chance to trigger predefined events at predefined, even recurring, times. This is accomplished by using the <CFSCHEDULE> tag that has the following basic format:

```
<CFSCHEDULE ACTION="Update"
  TASK="taskName"
  OPERATION="HTTPRequest"
  STARTDATE="Date"
  STARTTIME="Time"
  URL="templateFile"
  INTERVAL="Seconds">
```

- **Action** is the type of scheduled event, which can be update, run and delete. Update adds or changes a scheduled task and uses various other parameters. Delete removes a task from the scheduler and Run triggers the task immediately. Delete and Run only require a task name to work.
- **Task** is the name of the scheduled task. This is used to refer to the task in administrator and in any <CFSCHEDULE> tags that want to manipulate the task. You need a unique name for every unique task.
- **Operation**. In the current version the only type of task you can have here is the HTTPRequest operation.
- **StartDate** is a date object that refers to the first date on which the task is to be executed.
- **StartTime** is a time object that refers to the time on the above date that the task is executed.
- **URL** is the address of the page that is to be executed. This is just a standard template file but as a user never directly views it does not need to generate any output.
- **Interval** is the time that the task waits, in seconds, until it runs again.

There are various other attributes that can be added such as to set end times for the tasks or to run password protected URLs.

For this example we will create a task that simply counts the number of hits that our site has had up until now, and then emails us with the result. We could generate many complex reports to send, but we will stick to this simple one at the moment to understand the mechanics. Create a new directory called schedule off your *wwwroot* and save the following template as *emailme.cfm:*

```
<HTML>
<HEAD>
	<TITLE>MailTest</TITLE>
</HEAD>
<BODY>
<CFQUERY name="report" datasource="MyLog">
```

```
    Select * from Log
</CFQUERY>
<CFMAIL TO="person@readers.net"
  FROM="person@readers.net"
  SUBJECT="Website Daily Report"
  SERVER="mail.isp.net"
    PORT="25">
    <CFOUTPUT>
        This is an automated email from your
        website. The reports have been run
        at #Now()# and
        you have had #report.recordcount#
        hits to the site so far.
    </CFOUTPUT>
</CFMAIL>
</BODY>
</HTML>
```

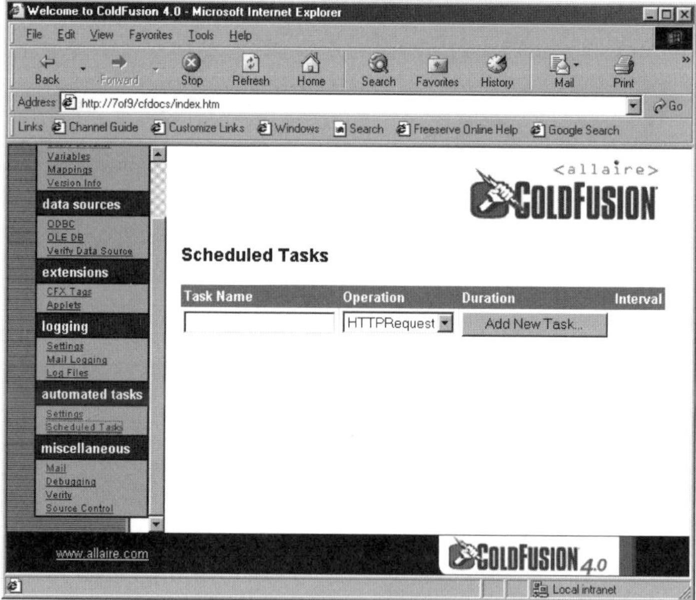

Figure 16.1 – An empty task list.

Now we have the task we need to drop it into our scheduler. Before we do this we need to have a look at what ColdFusion has plans to do at the moment.

Load a web browser and go to the CFDOCS directory on your web server. Once there, scroll down until you see the ColdFusion Administrator link and click on that. After you have logged in (you did write the password down earlier didn't you?) you will see the navigation bar down the left hand side of the page. Figure 16.1 shows the screen that you will see when you click on the **Scheduled Tasks** link on the navigation bar.

Figure 16.1 shows what is currently being scheduled on the system. If the ColdFusion server is a development system and not shared it is unlikely that there will be any tasks scheduled. You can use the ColdFusion Administrator to add and edit tasks here, but these can also be done via template files and the <CFSCHEDULE> tag. We will use the latter to schedule our email report to trigger at 11:30pm every evening. To add the task we will need the following template file saved as *createtask.cfm* in your *schedule* directory:

```
<HTML>
<HEAD>
      <TITLE>Add email Task</TITLE>
</HEAD>
<BODY>
<CFSCHEDULE ACTION="Update"
  TASK="test1"
  OPERATION="HTTPRequest"
  STARTDATE="#CreateODBCDate(CreateDate(2000, 8, 30))#"
  STARTTIME="#CreateODBCTime(CreateTime(23, 30, 00))#"
  URL="emailme.cfm"
  INTERVAL="86400">
</BODY>
</HTML>
```

Most of the above template file is straightforward apart from the start time and date. We have to create a ColdFusion date and time object but then turn it into an ODBC time object for it to remain compatible with the scheduling timer.

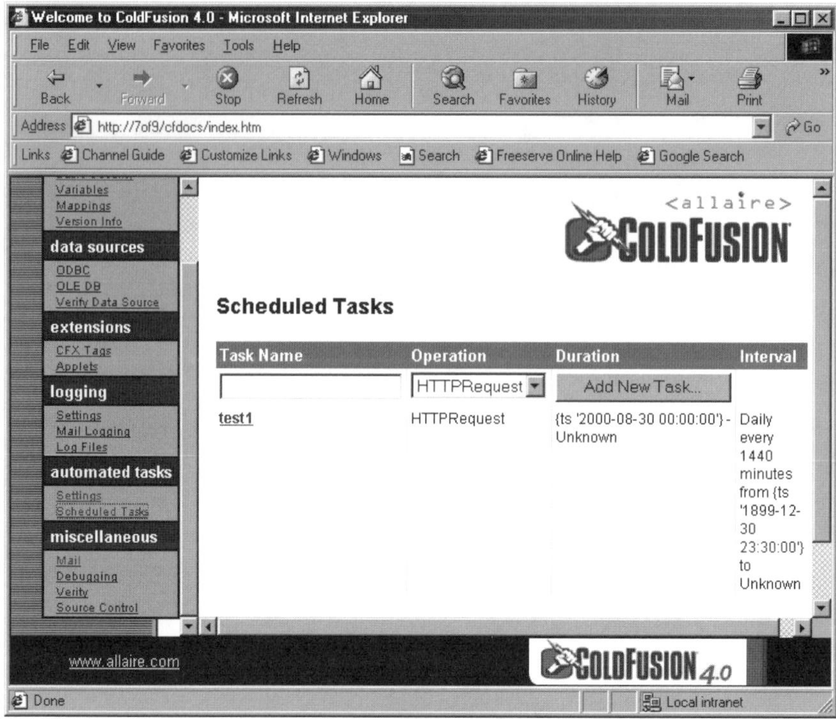

Figure 16.2 – The new task added with the CFSCHEDULE tag.

Minimize the Administrator Web browser and open a new browser window. Point your browser at the *createtask.cfm* file. The output should just be an empty web page, but the task should now be submitted to the scheduler.

To check this switch to the ColdFusion Administrator browser window again and click on the Scheduled Tasks link in the navigation bar again. This forces the page to refresh. Figure 16.2 shows the new page with your task added. At 11:30 each night this task will be executed if the server is turned on. If there are any errors in the scheduled tasks these can be found in the file *\cfusion\log\schedule.log* on your web server.

<CFSCHEDULE> can also be used to generate static pages from dynamic query pages. If you had a huge database that many users throughout the day had to

perform the same query on, it would be more resource efficient to perform the query once, and show everyone the same result set. <CSSCHEDULE> can be used to do this – consult the ColdFusion Manuals for more information on this function.

Chapter

17

The ColdFusion Fast Web Site

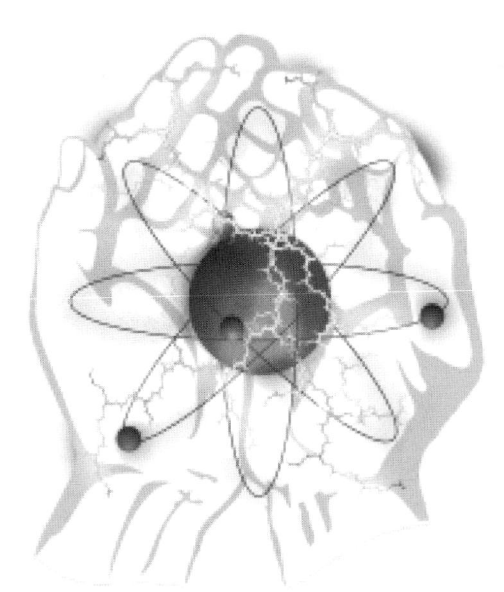

Introduction

To demonstrate some of the concepts that have been described in this book the following web site has been set up:

http://www.coldfusionfast.com

Figure 17.1 shows the front page of this site. This chapter gives you background information about the site, its mechanics and navigation and how to use it.

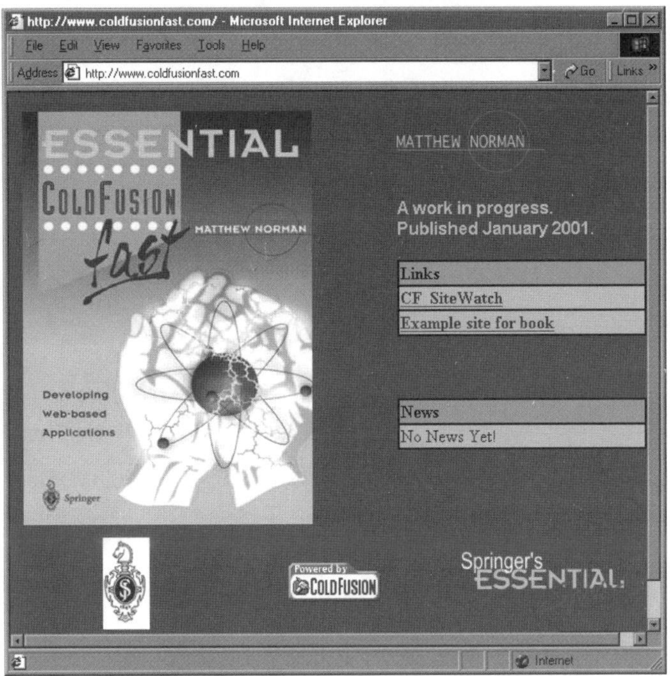

Figure 17.1 – http://www.coldfusionfast.com.

The main page, which is shown in figure 17.1 is your entrance to the site. You can use this to go and find out about ColdFusion, about Springer, the publishers of the book, and the Essential Series in general. Click on the author's name to visit his web site and see what he really looks like!

ShowMe button

***Figure 17.2** – The ShowMe Button.*

Figure 17.2 shows the ShowMe button. On the ColdFusion *fast* web site every page will have this button on it. If you click on this button this will show the ColdFusion template that has been used to create the file.

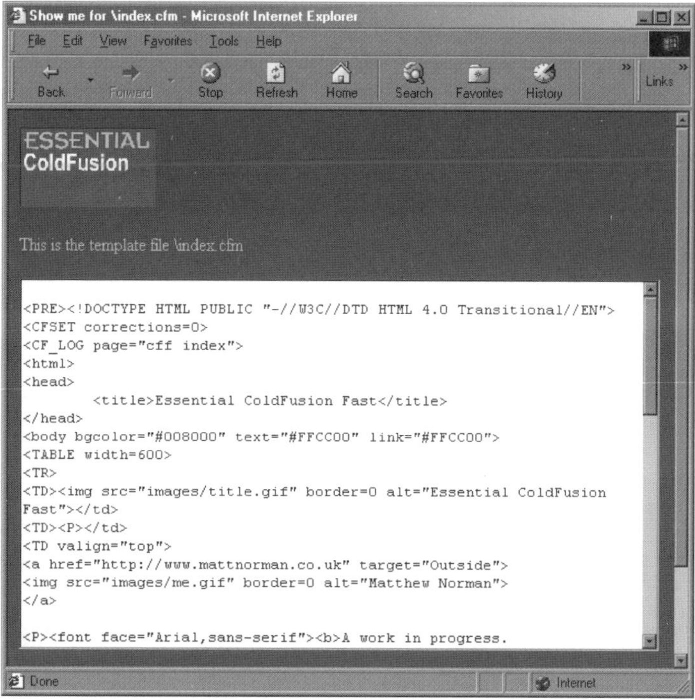

***Figure 17.3** – ShowMe results for the first page.*

Figure 17.3 shows the results of clicking on this button on the first page. You can scroll up and down looking at the code and copy it into your own files if required.

News

The news link on the main page will contain any news or information about ColdFusion and the book, or any other pertinent points. Headlines will be shown on the main page and clicking on the headline will reveal the full text of the news item. The news and the headlines are stored in a table in the datasource called news, which stores the body and the headlines and the date submitted to the system. The page that displays the stories will list all of the headlines if no news ID field is provided via the URL, or will display the specific story if the StoryID is provided. All of this functionality is provided within one template file. Click on the ShowMe icon to see it. No web-based method of submitting the new items is provided for security.

Sitewatch

CF_Sitewatch is an application that stores details of ColdFusion servers that people have found on the web. This is hoped to become a database that everyone can enter URLs into when they find a ColdFusion server or spot a *.cfm* file in a URL.

A user to the site submits a URL in a similar way to making an entry in the visitor's book described in an earlier chapter. When a user logs an entry the entry is stored with a moderated flag and an email is sent to the webmaster. The webmaster then goes away and views the site submitted and if it can be verified as a ColdFusion site removes the moderated flag. At this point the site is viewable on the sitewatch page and the submitting user, if they have provided an email address, is thanked for their help with an email.

If you find a ColdFusion site on the Internet come and log its URL so we can watch how this product is being used throughout the world. If you administer a ColdFusion site please log it via CF_Sitewatch yourself.

Book Site

The book site section contains all of the source code described in this book as live examples that you can run.

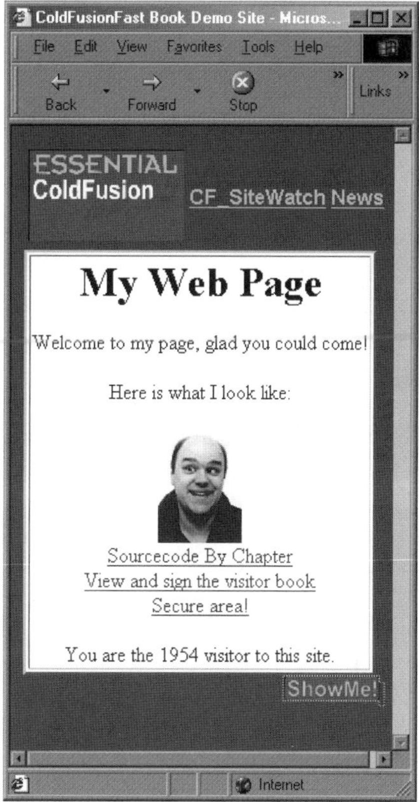

Figure 17.4 – The homepage of our example web site.

The pages are divided into chapters so you can easily locate your code. The datasource name is different to that described in the book and some functionality of the code, such as the <CFMAIL> tags, have been disabled to prevent anyone sending too much mail.

On the occasions where we have developed a template file over several different evolutions the last working version of the file will be stored on the book site.

If any of the examples asks for a password, have a look at the source code in this book to see what the password is. No real explanation of the code is given on the web site, as that is what this book is for. The web site has been provided to demonstrate the code if you do not have access to a ColdFusion server and to make it easier for you to type it in if you do.

Main Page

Figure 17.4 shows the front page of the book site section, which is the index page of the site that we have been describing throughout the book. The additions are links to other sections of this example web site.

Administration area

The administration area is equivalent to our secure area in the previous chapter. The passwords are in the example templates in the chapter. From this area you can list some of the accesses to the site, and look at individual visitor book entries. You are not allowed to delete entries – that is the job of the webmaster.

Visitor Book

Figure 17.5 shows the visitor book section of the site, where users can log their access to the site as described in the text, and see other's comments.

Figure 17.5 – The visitor book page

Our final chapter will deal with some of the other places that you can turn to for help with using ColdFusion.

Chapter

18 Additional Resources

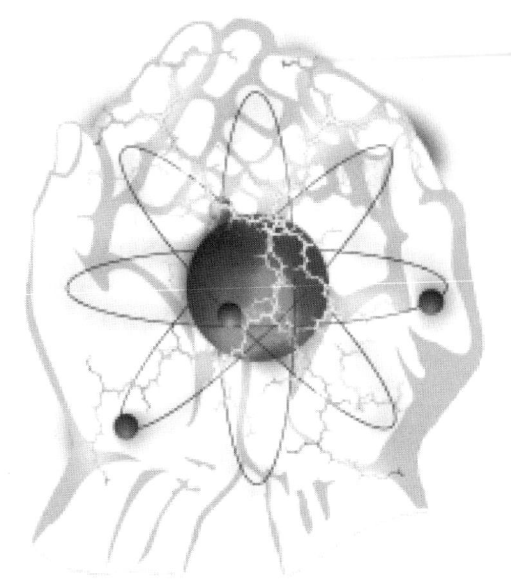

Introduction

No book can cover every eventuality of using a piece of complex software and still remain readable and usable. This final chapter will discuss some of the options that you have for getting more help with using ColdFusion.

Manuals and CFDOCS

One of the most annoying comments that is made to a computer user with a problem is, 'read the manual.' Unfortunately that is just what this section is going to suggest to you. However, the author has been consistently surprised with the quality and the helpfulness of the documentation that you get with the ColdFusion product. Most of the problems that you encounter while developing ColdFusion applications can be answered by looking in the *CFML Language Reference Manual* and the *Developing Web Applications with ColdFusion Manual.* The author would highly recommend these manuals and feels that they are some of the best documentation available.

One point to note about these manuals is that they overlap, but don't neglect looking in both of the manuals for information about your problem. For instance, take the <CFMAIL> tag. If you have a problem with this tag look it up in the *Language Reference* to familiarize yourself with its syntax. If that does not answer your question, use the index at the back of the *Developing Web Applications with ColdFusion Manual* and check what that has to say. Although the *Language Reference Manual* shows you examples in a clinical fashion, the other manual gives you more general tips on its use.

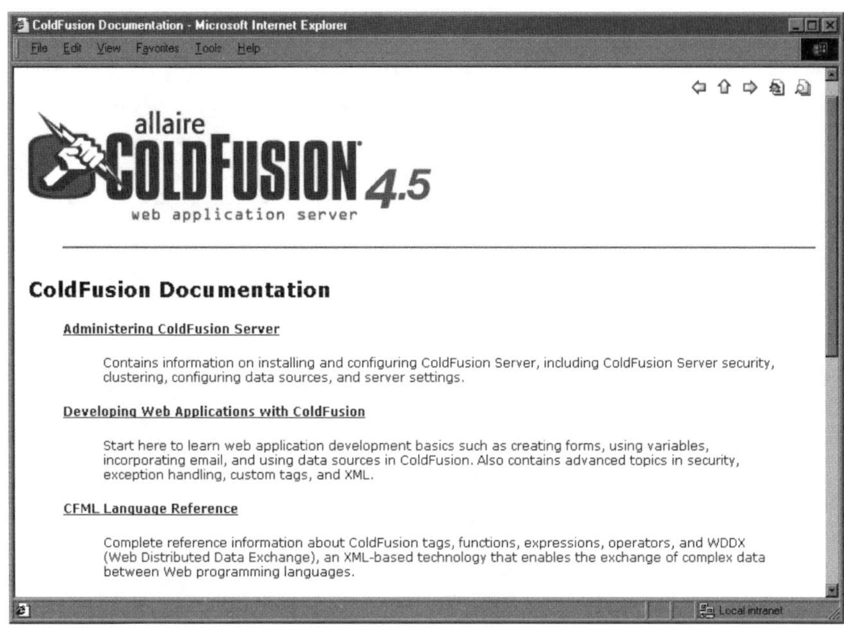

Figure 18.1 – Web based manual and documentation files.

Figure 18.1 shows the *cfdocs* directory that ColdFusion placed on your web server at install time. This is another useful resource and is a direct copy of the data in the manuals. The exception to this is if you have upgraded ColdFusion at any time. When you upgrade, or apply a patch, you have the option to upgrade your documentation set. There is also an errata and additions section to the documentation that can be viewed via the web.

One further advantage of the online documentation is that they can also run the examples live. This is also a great way of learning about the product. Due to their electronic nature you can also search the documentation by clicking on the magnifying glass icon at the top of the screen.

ColdFusion Studio

ColdFusion Studio is an HTML and CFML editor. Although the author feels that this is not a necessity for developing in ColdFusion, it is a luxury that will help you to develop your web site faster. Figure 18.2 shows a screenshot of Studio editing a template file. Studio is very similar to other products, such as Microsoft's FrontPage, yet it is enhanced by the inclusion of CFML support and documentation. Again if you upgrade the version of ColdFusion Server you are using you can get additional document packs for Studio without having to upgrade that as well.

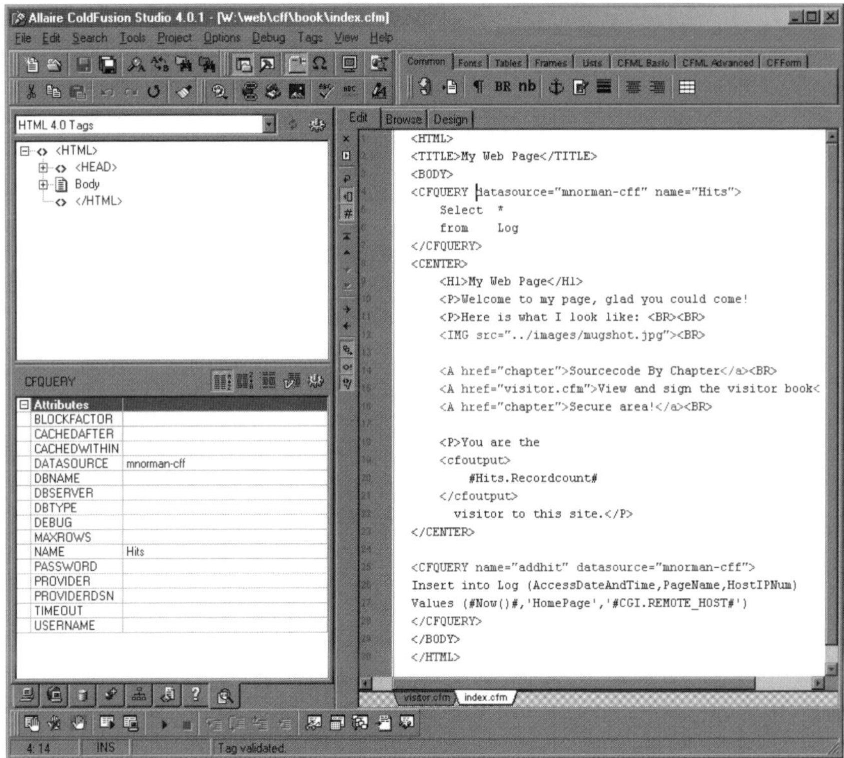

Figure 18.2 – ColdFusion Studio editing a template file.

Figure 18.2 shows the attribute list for <CFQUERY> and if you type values into this area it automatically appends them to the template file, which is a useful reminder. Studio can also interface directly with the ColdFusion server to obtain information about datasources and table names. You can also create projects which are sets of template files and even graphically show the links between them as in Figure 18.3.

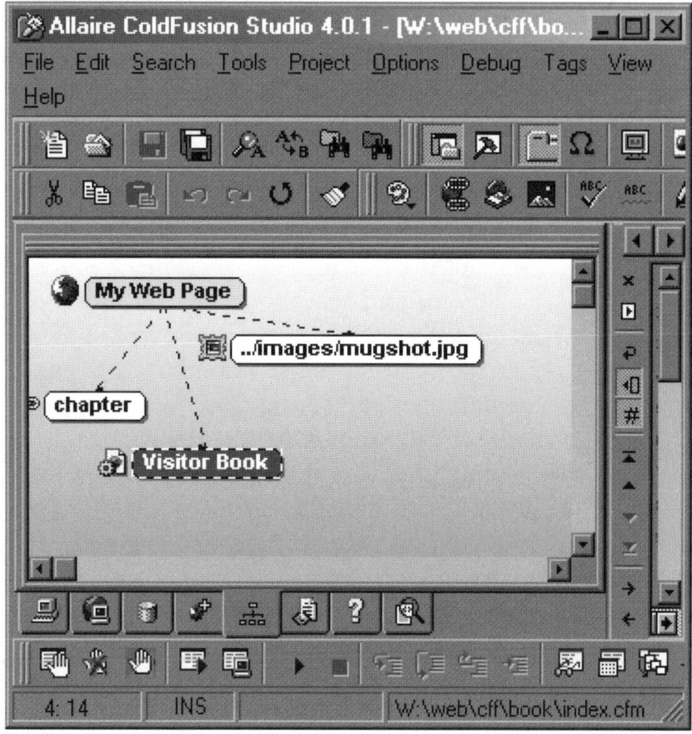

Figure 18.3 – A Studio project will diagram your web site.

While discussing ColdFusion Studio, Macromedia Dreamweaver also deserves mentioning. This product is also aware of *.cfm* files and can process some of CFML. Since the announced merger of Allaire and Macromedia it is likely that Dreamweaver will be developed further to support ColdFusion programming.

ColdFusion Developer Exchange

Chapter 13 introduced you to the concept of custom tags; small portable pieces of code that could be reused. Allaire has set up a web site that allows users to share the custom tags that they have created with other developers. This web site can be found at:

http://www.allaire.com/developer/

If you are developing an application and suddenly need a piece of code that, for instance, obtains a list of all the email addresses on a given web site, then it is likely that someone has written a custom tag that will do it for you. Figure 18.4 shows an example page from this site. Some of the tags are free to use, others can be bought from the site. Some of the free tags are encrypted, which means you can run them, and use them, but not view or edit the code inside them. Other tags are just like ones you have created yourself, and can be modified as you want. If you find a tag that does something close to what you want, then there is the chance to modify it to make it exactly what you need.

Remember that areas like this are not just for the taking. If you create a wonderful custom tag that others could use, you may wish to share it with the rest of the ColdFusion community.

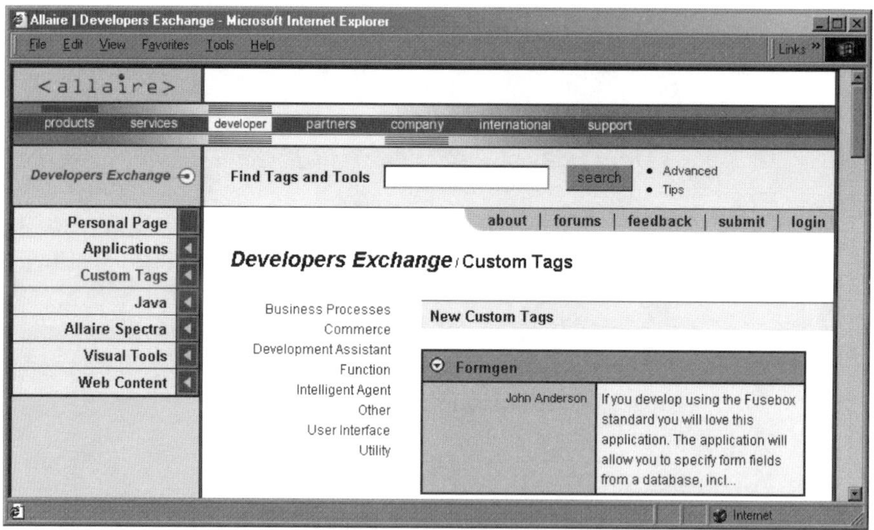

Figure 18.4 – Custom tags area of the development exchange.

ColdFusion Forums

Another useful area of the Allaire web site can be found at:

http://www.allaire.com/DEVELOPER/ReferenceDesk/Forums.cfm

This is the forum area where developers with problems, questions or tips can share them with the rest of the community. If there is a pressing problem with your code you may like to post your question to the forum. While you are there you may even look at some of the questions and answers that others have raised, and maybe even be able to help sort their problems out.

Figure 18.5 – Developer forums

Figure 18.5 shows a list of various topics that are being discussed at the time of writing.

When you post a question it is displayed to everyone else as shown in figure 18.6.

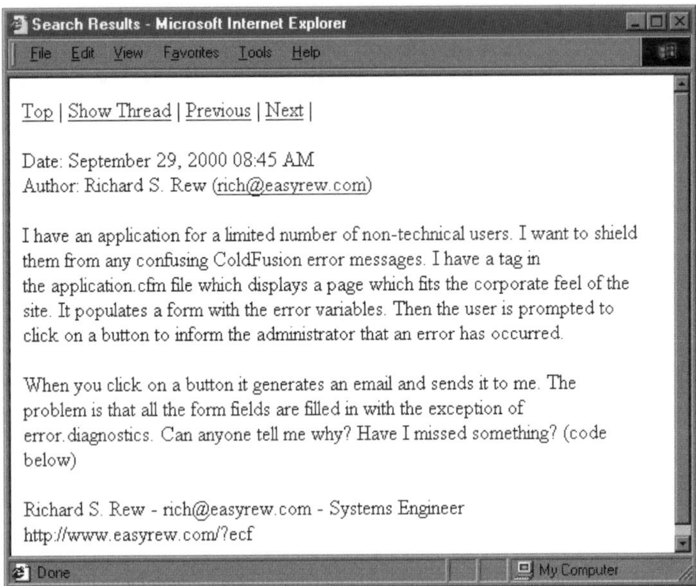

Figure 18.6 *- A developer forum question.*

Final Words

If you are really stuck with a problem do not forget to search the web generally for an answer. Search engines like *www.google.com* are invaluable for finding bits of information about ColdFusion. It may be that someone has put a solution to your problem on their web site and a few choice words placed into a search engine can hunt them down.

The Allaire site also has lists of ColdFusion user groups, so you may be able to network with other like-minded individuals and share experiences and problems with them.

Index

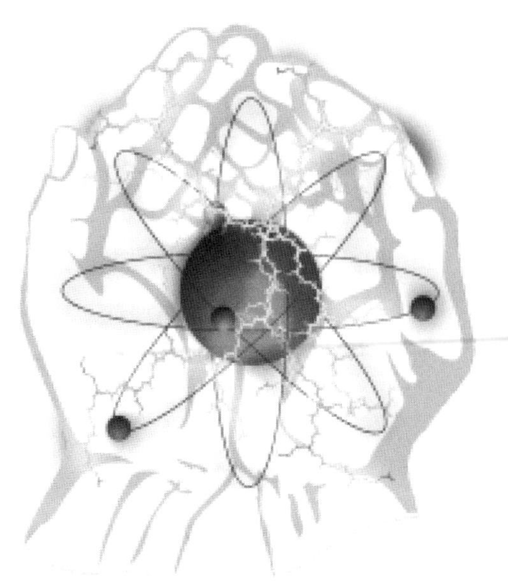

A

B

C

L

M

N

O

P

Q

R

S

T

U

V

Essential Flash 5.0 *fast*

Fiaz Hussain

Learn to create imaginative and lively animation for the web with **Essential Flash 5.0 *fast***!

The latest release of Macromedia's Flash, version 5.0, adds new features to the popular web applications software - such as enhanced colour controls, better selection highlights, draggable guides, pen tool, shared libraries, new panels, and expanded ActionScript capabilities.

Fiaz Hussain tells you about:

- The Flash development environment;
- The creation of simple and complex objects;
- The shape editing tools and colour;
- Symbols and their instances;
- Layers and animation;
- Interactivity, including ActionScripting; and
- How to optimise Flash movies for fast downloads.

Focusing on the important components required to get started using Flash quickly, this book shows you all the tips and techniques you need to create your own Web applications, *fast*.

280 pages
Softcover
ISBN 1-85233-451-7

Please see page 265 for ordering details

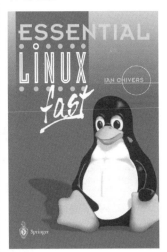